ALLISTER ('ASHIE') BREBNE   ass
tenement near Pittodrie Sta   15
and trained as a motor veh   in-
tenance engineer in Aberde   he
explosion of outdoor activity after 1945, Ashie developed a deep
love of the Scottish mountains and in 1963 gave up his job and
co-founded Highland Safaris, a nature and outdoor guiding
company, which he continued with until his retirement. Ashie lives
in Strathpeffer, Ross-shire and this is his first book.

Beyond the Secret Howff

ASHIE BREBNER

Luath Press Limited
EDINBURGH
www.luath.co.uk

First published 2017
Reprinted 2018

ISBN: 978-1-910745-87-8

The paper used in this book is recyclable. It is made from
low chlorine pulps produced in a low energy, low emissions manner
from renewable forests.

Printed and bound by
Bell & Bain Ltd., Glasgow

Typeset in 10.5 point Sabon
by 3btype.com

For Norma, Derry and Bruce,
who put up with my long absences
every summer over many years.

Contents

Acknowledgements

I owe a great debt to Ian R Mitchell for his encouragement, constructive criticism and initial editing, without which this book would never have been written. But most of all, for the friendship which developed through our mutual love of the wild places of the Scottish Highlands.

Introduction

I HAD HEARD OF, or rather read of, Ashie long before I met him. In 'Cairngorm Commentary', my favourite chapter of the great Aberdonian mountaineer Tom Patey's classic book, *One Man's Mountains*, there was a reference to the various underbelly characters who frequented the Cairngorms in the 1950s – a full decade before I myself ventured there. Just as was the case later in the 1960s, everybody ten years before had had a nickname and here were, amongst many others, Chesty, Dizzie, Sticker... and Ashie. Patey had introduced me to Ashie, but in doing so had made an error; in the same chapter he ascribed the building of the Secret Howff on Beinn a' Bhuird (which was a home from home for me in the 1960s) to another group of climbers, the Kincorth Club, whose *leader-aff* was one Freddy Malcolm.

I had inadvertently perpetuated Patey's error, by repeating it in a chapter of the work I co-wrote with Dave Brown in the late 1980s, *Mountain Days and Bothy Nights*, and there the matter rested... until, after a further decade had passed, Ashie was given a copy of our book. He had already discovered that his howff still existed and was being maintained, and to put the matter straight he wrote to me with a full account of the construction of this 'Eighth Wonder of the Cairngorms' (Patey), which is reproduced in this current volume.

Ashie and I became good pals and met and communicated over the years many times, and collaborated on a number of radio and television programmes as well. Just a pity he is that bit *ower auld tae keep up wi mi on the hills*, or I am sure we would have also been mountaineering buddies. Seriously though, Ashie helped me in other ways, in addition to the finer points of Cairngorm mountaineering historiography, in that he was a great boon to my writing of the volume I published on our mutual home city, *Aberdeen Beyond the Granite*, by giving me fascinating information about the part of Aberdeen – its Grunnit Heart – where he grew up. I was thus more than willing to give Ashie a hand in turn by writing an Introduction to his book.

But again and again, it was more than that. Our whole generation of the 1960s owed so much to Ashie's pioneering post-war mountaineering companions. They pioneered the climbing routes that were in the Guidebooks by the time we emerged, they wore down the resistance of the lairds and others who were hostile to the accessing of the hills – thus, by our day, though still there, that was a residual problem. And by using the houses of the gamekeepers, shepherds and others that were being abandoned from around 1940, they started the whole bothy tradition, which also ensured that by using them, the buildings were still there when the Mountain Bothies Association, like the Seventh Cavalry, came to their rescue from 1965 onwards.

Ashie's tale is not unique; it is a part of the wider story of the discovery of the mountaineering outdoors by the working class of Scotland. It started first on Clydeside in the 1930s with the onset of the depression, and its tale is embodied in accounts of the lives of such people as Jock Nimlim, which has been told by IDS Thomson in *May the Fire Always Be Lit*. Aberdeen, up there in the Caul Shulder of the country was, as often, slower to respond, but in the aftermath of 1945, it caught up with seven league ex-Army boots. As Ashie says, the availability of cheap ex-Army gear was an essential element in facilitating the activities of young working men in the era of post war austerity. And these were days of broadening horizons: full employment and gradually increasing leisure time gave people opportunities for outdoor activities their Depression-hit parents could not have dreamed of. But Ashie and his peers were less fortunate than we – who came so shortly later – were in one way; they missed out on the phenomenal expansion of education, free education, that we had, and most of them had to remain in industrial or other employment. By the 1960s anyone with intelligence could do a couple of evening classes, go to university on a full grant with no fees – and no risk – jobs a plenty were a-waiting for graduates then. Almost all of the working class kids I went to the hills with in the 1960s were manual workers, like Ashie, often serving an apprenticeship. But all of them escaped from industrial wage slavery through university. Ashie's generation? Some – like Freddy Malcolm – remained industrial workers, some, like Chesty and Sticker, emigrated to Canada and elsewhere, but only one, Ashie himself, took the road he did.

And taking that road took courage; he took a big risk, giving up a steady job in the Never Had It So Good era of the early 1960s, and heading off like a pioneer into a Highlands where no one offered, and no one had tried to offer, mountain guiding and nature guiding. Ashie had, the reader will see, a strong personality, and support from his life-partner. He is also a man of some skill: self-taught ski mountaineer, self-taught ornithologist. And, as I discovered when working through his manuscript, an excellent self-taught writer, a product of the days *fan ye were learned richt at the squeel* – and belted if you made mistakes!

Recently, by writing a couple of articles in journals and appearing on a number of radio and TV programmes, Ashie has become a kind of cult figure amongst the cognoscenti of the Scottish mountaineering world. The publication of *Beyond the Secret Howff* will bring a wider audience of contemporary mountaineers, skiers and naturalists to Allister Brebner's engrossing tales of adventures in a Highlands far removed from today's touristified mecca. Readers will enjoy his tales of early bothying and pioneering mountain skiing, of building the Secret Howff, and of his later experiences and adventures in the Highlands at a period that now seems very remote. Ashie has been able, within the limitations we all face, to live the kind of life he wanted to live. How many of us can say that?

I did, I suppose, inevitably, read these biographical essays with a certain nostalgia, but also with a sense of sadness. The social changes we have witnessed in society since, for the sake of argument, the 1980s, have meant that the world is not producing the Ashies and the Chestys and the Stickers any more, any more than it is producing the Fishgut Macs and Stumpys of my 1960s generation. The idea that someone from Ashie's background could do today what he did then, is preposterous, as preposterous as is the idea that the housing estate in Aberdeen where I grew up could send, as it did in the 1960s, dozens of kids to university every year. Ashie ends his book by welcoming the expansion of outdoor activities and nature education and other factors that have brought countless thousands to experience the life of the Scottish mountains. Alas – though age can dim perspective as well as eyesight and hearing – these developments have brought with them a certain blandness. For that reason, as well as for its intrinsic qualities, I thoroughly recommend Ashie's book to any reader interested in the Scottish outdoors.

Ian R Mitchell

Tied to The Machine: Early Life in Aberdeen

IT WAS SPRING 1963. The machinery clattered incessantly and the heat was oppressive as I stared dispiritedly out of the factory window. Surely there must be another way of making a living? I had been working here for six years now as a maintenance mechanic for the machines, which produced countless thousands of envelopes every day. I loathed it and felt trapped. There was a family tradition of working here. My three aunts had spent all their working lives in the factory. Their potential husbands had in all probability been killed in the First World War. My father, too, had resigned himself to a lifetime here. He had contracted rheumatic fever as a prisoner of war towards the end of the same conflict and, after six long years of unemployment, had been grateful for the opportunity of secure work. He was not at all eager that I should do the same.

I had served an apprenticeship as a motor mechanic, not for any great love of motor vehicles but because a job was available and there was nothing else worthwhile to do. It was usually the case that the garages at that time would employ several apprentices (for they were useful cheap labour) and then at the end of a five-year period, the apprentices' employment would be terminated, usually when the winter came along. It may be difficult to believe now but most people who could afford a car in the early 1950s would lay up their car during the winter months, so with no repairs needed to cars, the garage was empty and the employer would pay off the fully fledged apprentices to save money – and you would have to look around for something else. Hence the reason for my employment in the envelope making factory.

This was Pirie Appleton's works in central Aberdeen, just beside the Joint Station, and it employed about 500 workers at that time. Pirie's had originally been a cotton mill, later it converted to the paper industry. It was crammed into a narrow location beside the station, and was a notable landmark in the town centre in the 1950s and '60s, since on one gable wall there was a huge representation of a Scottie Dog as an advertising logo; the mill has long since closed and has been replaced by an ugly office block.

My first position in this job was to maintain all the pulleys, shafts and belts over six floors of clattering machines, which produced all shapes, sizes and qualities of envelope. There were on each floor approximately up to 160 machines in four rows of shafts ranged over the six floors. I was kitted out in a specially designed boiler suit which was very close fitting, especially around the sleeves and cuffs, for this was potentially a dangerous job. Since it was impossible to hear any sound other than the clatter of machinery, a coloured light would come on which would alert me to a problem on a particular floor. I would make my way to the trouble spot and find that a machine was giving trouble, and there a mechanic specialising in this type of machine would be waiting for me. Since he couldn't work on it while the pulley and belt were still running off the main shaft, it was my job to throw the belt off the main driving shaft for the whole department. This way the machine could be isolated without the entire department of perhaps 160 machines being brought to a halt. This is where the specialised boiler suit came in, for I had to pull the belt off at the machine end to allow the mechanic to work safely, then climb atop the machine on completion of the work, to throw the belt back on to the spinning main pulley shaft, making sure I was on the right side of the fast spinning pulley, then throw the belt on quickly. If any part of my attire caught on the belts, then at least I would be thrown out. There had been many fatalities of people being dragged in by throwing the belt from the wrong side.

All these individual machines were operated by women. In fact, it was a major source of employment for women in Aberdeen and quite early on I discovered an anomaly and a puzzle which took me some time to work out. While waiting for the mechanic to finish a repair, I fell into conversation with the girl who operated it. I had heard that this girl had just got married, so I bawled out, 'I hear ye got mairriet last week!'

She looked all around her in horror and said into my ear, 'For God's sake, dinna spikk about that in here! If the bosses hear aboot that, I'm oot the door!'

'Foo is that then?' I asked, mystified.

'Because mairriet women are nae allowed tae work here,' was the answer.

This greatly puzzled me at the time. It seemed a strange order from above for why would they prevent a potentially good worker from being employed simply because they were married? Then the answer came to me and was well illustrated in my own family. Far from being a diktat, it was an act of compassion. After two world wars, because there were so many single women whose potential husbands had been killed, it had been decided that single women would be given top priority of work, for in those days married women could expect a husband's support. This had happened in my own family. My father had four unmarried sisters. One volunteered to be housekeeper while the other three obtained work at the envelope factory. This way, they each reached the position of head of a department at the end of their working lives and maintained a reasonably good standard of living.

The factory faced onto a busy Aberdeen street. How I envied all those people outside in comparative freedom while I was chained to these dreadful machines. If it weren't for weekends, I would most certainly have gone under long ago. Fortunately, I had discovered the Cairngorms and the North West Highlands before I left school and it was immediately apparent that this was where I belonged. This was mainly thanks to a far sighted technical teacher at Frederick Street School. Jim Moir was a very keen hill man who thought it good for us town kids to get a taste of the real outdoors and took a group of us on a climb of Clachnaben on Lower Deeside near Banchory and also Bennachie to the north of

Aberdeen. I was immediately hooked. Though I had been born and bred in the town, it was only in the hills that I felt truly alive. Through a long and dreary apprenticeship, every weekend was spent in the blissful freedom of the hills. It was my only escape but however I racked my brain, there seemed no way I could earn a living in the mountains.

I was born in 1935 in a flat on the top floor of a working-class tenement in Seaforth Road in Aberdeen. This was in the heart of the area where Aberdeen's granite industry was located, and that was still a big employer at that time, though it has gone the way of most of Aberdeen's industry – paper mills, trawling and others, into oblivion. I had two elder brothers, George, six years my senior and Albert eight years older. My early life was dominated by the Second World War. An early memory is waking up under my mother's arm (her other arm was holding the family documents in a cardboard box) and being bumped down the common stairs in a great rush to the air raid shelter as the siren sounded. The shelter took up the whole back garden and was built to house the six families of the tenement. There was no sense of deprivation in those wartime days, for you just accept the world you are born into. Our tenement was on the whole a very happy place, the centre one in a block of five solid granite buildings. Each tenement was divided into two and three room flats on either side of a central stairway. On each landing was a lavatory which was shared by two tenants. The flats had no bathrooms but had a scullery where all the cooking and washing took place.

With a total of 30 families within the whole block, there was never a shortage of childhood friends. The summers were spent outdoors. We were well warned of the limits of our freedom, for there were lots of dangerous areas where the military were present, but this left a wide area, chief of which was the Broad Hill at the end of our street. This was at least 100ft high and a great adventure area for us – and to our eyes the perfect playground for our imagination. It had clear views in every direction. To the east lay the beach and North Sea and we could watch all the shipping movements entering and leaving the harbour to the south. To the west lay the familiar layout of Seaforth Road and its tenements, the whole area being dominated by a giant gasometer below which was Pittodrie Park, Aberdeen football team's home ground. To the north lay the River Don beyond which was an unknown land with a skyline of small areas of woodland with farmland beneath.

There were two events during this time which are engraved in my memory. The first being the visit of a policeman to our house and my mother in a very emotional state. Fearing an enemy landing on Aberdeen beach possibly launched from Norway, the whole of the beach and links were filled by bunkers, tank traps, barbed wire and crucially a large mined area. My brother George and pals were playing golf in the tiny area left to them when one hit a ball accidentally into a mined area which of course was wired off. The young lad whose ball it was crawled under the wire to retrieve it and stood on a mine which killed two or three pals, the full blast catching George on the face and blinding him. A brilliant eye surgeon named Souter spent years extracting steel and sand from his eyes and saved his sight. Though his eyes are still pitted he has good sight even yet.

The second memory is of the air raid on Aberdeen on 21 April 1943. I have no memory of the raid itself. I assume we were all in the shelter and I was told nothing of what happened close to our area in Powis and Causewayend (locally known as Casseyend), but I now know that 98 civilians and 27 soldiers were killed overnight. The news of what had happened had travelled quickly throughout the community next morning. My mother must have been very worried about a close friend who lived very near Casseyend and so next morning, since there was no one to look after me, she had to drag me along to discover if her friend was involved in the casualties. The friend was OK but I saw some of the damage that had been done chiefly to Causewayend church, the side of which had been ripped open, thus exposing the interior like a child's doll house. (The photograph is still reproduced in wartime Aberdeen books.

I must have been there around the same time as the photographer.) It made a very deep impression. (Perhaps I should add that when there were raids, my father, who was in the auxiliary fire service had to go down to Pirie Appleton and fire watch till the raid was over, so my mother had the responsibility of the family during this time).

On to better times. Once the war was over we had more freedom to spend any free time on the beach and the Broad Hill and we had very happy times there in winter, sledging when there was snow and in summer climbing the steeper east side as fast as we were able. We would watch the salmon cobbles go round the nets just off the beach and the prevailing sound of spring was that of the oystercatchers piping and wheeling over our heads. We spent far more time out of doors than children do over half a century later. You have to remember that TV only came to Aberdeen in 1956, that very few people could afford to own one, and that there was only one part-time channel! Staying in with your parents listening to the radio was boring, so you were out the door at every opportunity.

The streets were virtually traffic free in the 1950s and the street was our playground. And most of our games were group games, given that there were so many bairns about after the war. 'Kick the cannie' was one game; a can was kicked into the middle of the street and someone (who became IT) had to retrieve it and go search for the others who had hidden meanwhile, capturing them, whilst leaving the can in place. Anyone sneaking out and 'kicking the cannie' freed all the captives, and the game started again. This one could go on for hours, and did. Another game was called EIO – and it required a tennis ball. This was thrown against the gable end of the tenement block, the thrower nominating the person who was EIO (or IT). The others scattered but had to freeze when the nominated person caught the ball. He then threw it, and if hitting someone, that person in turn threw the ball against the wall, nominating another catcher, who in turn became IT, and so the game went on... and on... and on. But we were not the only ones playing games...

Strange things were happening on the Broad Hill around this time. Large numbers of men would appear from nowhere and they would gather in large groups. What their purpose was, we couldn't quite understand, for we were always told to clear off if we came anywhere near them – and even our parents told us not to approach them. It was all very mysterious. Then occasionally, the police would appear and everyone would disappear very quickly. It was only some time later that we realised that what we were witnessing was the operation of a very large gambling school. It took some time for the police to sort it out and we had our hill back again.

From our top flat on a Saturday we could hear the great roar from Pittodrie as the home side, Aberdeen FC, scored a goal. Aberdeen FC – 'The Dons' – were doing well at that time, winning their first Scottish Cup in 1947 and then the League in 1955. For me it was always more fun to actually play the game than watch it so I had no inclination to go into the stadium, but the streets around the area were usually filled by fans going to or leaving a match. There was one slightly frightening occasion when a pal and I were at the Castlegate just after the end of an important game. We were waiting for a tram to take us to somewhere, I cannot now recall where. As we waited, the area suddenly filled with fans leaving the game and when a tramcar came along, we were lifted bodily off our feet and carried forward as the crowd surged. Luckily for us, a few men surrounding us saw our predicament and pushed everyone away but it was a very frightening moment when you realised you had no control.

I moved up to Frederick Street Secondary School in 1946. It was a fairly relaxed time. The school playfields, when we were allowed to use them, lay on the links between the Corporation Gasworks and the ICI chemical works, so goodness knows what we were breathing in at the time. We had been taught mainly by elderly women teachers in primary, the male schoolteachers being off to war. Now they returned and in the main were more interested in telling their wartime tales than knocking any sense into us. There were one or two exceptions. One such was Jim Moir, already mentioned. We didn't realise it at the time but he was much more of an outdoor man. We didn't know anything existed outside Aberdeen but he helped to put this right by taking a group of us to Clachnaben on Lower Deeside. It opened my eyes to a wider world and its possibilities. He – I think – deliberately took us the long way over the top of Mount Shade, down the far side then up the other, probably in an attempt to slow us down a little, but I still remember the exhilaration of running full tilt all the way down from Clachnaben.

A second expedition took us out to Bennachie. It must have been spring for there were showers drifting across the landscape. My chief memory on the summit was watching the showers leave the cloud and drift across the Aberdeenshire farmland, something I had never experienced before. In Seaforth Road it was either raining or it wasn't. I decided then, this is where I wanted to be. I was to meet Jim Moir very briefly many years later but that lay far in the future. Ian Mitchell, also an Aberdonian, and aware of where I had spent my early years, drew my attention many years later to *Amande's Bed*, a novel by John Aberdein. He had been brought up in the same area as I, albeit a decade later, and it described his early life as the son of a committed Communist Party activist. It was an excellent read with all the real characters I'd known as a child thinly disguised and brought to life again, teachers, neighbours – and even the local shopkeepers! It had the effect of re-enforcing all the memories of a very happy childhood.

I left school at 15 and after a year of training at a pre-apprenticeship school, started my apprenticeship with Rossleigh Ltd, agents for Jaguar and Rover. The idea of any further education was never mentioned, but many years later I learned from my mother that my eldest brother had passed the examinations for Gray's School of Art in the city, and might have been eligible for a bursary to attend. However, this required my father going through a 'means test' to see if my brother Albert was eligible for financial help. Possibly with memories in his mind of the Means Test of the 1930s and the humiliation that had involved for those subject to it, my father refused to comply. So began my working life for the next decade or more.

Here is a strange thing. In the earliest days after leaving school and making new friends in the tiny climbing world of the time, it was natural for us to continue our friendship during the normal working week. There was not a great deal to do in Aberdeen if you had very little money and were too young to go into a pub of an evening. The only alternative appeared to be the cinema and there was a wide choice here with much more interesting films than those made today. (Despite not managing to get to Art School, my brother Albert initially became an illustrator working on the advertising posters for the cinema in Aberdeen, mostly then owned by the Donald family who also owned Aberdeen FC.) However, the 'pictures', as we called them, were not satisfactory, for we couldn't discuss the last weekend or the next. Someone came up with a cheap alternative: snooker.

There was a large snooker hall directly above Collies the grocer on Union Street, famous for the wonderful smell of coffee which percolated from its premises. The problem was that snooker was regarded as the Devil's Work at the time. No good would come of you if you idled your hours away on such a terrible past-time, our elders said. I can't imagine what our betters thought we got up to there. So the practice was to pretend to be slowly passing by, have a quick look up and down Union Street to see if there was anyone we recognised, and to slip in quickly and spend the evening wickedly playing snooker and planning the next weekend in the hills. That was becoming my real passion.

CHAPTER ONE

The Post-war Birth of Cairngorm Bothying

I WAS INTRODUCED to mountaineering in the changed days after the Second World War, and one of the greatest changes was the emergence of the tradition of bothying, especially in the Cairngorms. Bothies were old gamekeepers', shepherds' or sometimes foresters' houses, which were gradually being abandoned from about 1940 onwards, providing a new source of accommodation in the great outdoors. And for us of limited means, for whom even youth hostels were an expensive luxury, they had the great advantage of being free.

I think my first experience of a bothy was probably around 1949 at the Spittal of Glenmuick where Jock Robertson would allow walkers and climbers to use a barn for an overnight stay and as a base for climbing on Lochnagar or walking over to the Angus Glens. Jock, the keeper for Glenmuick, was a very amiable person who had a good relationship with the climbing fraternity and as a very young lad, I well remember how Jock walked on the hill. While we raced on and then stopped for a rest, we would look back and see him with his steady, measured stride, plodding relentlessly up the path without ever stopping. He covered the ground as fast as we did with our quick dashes and rests and we soon realised this was how you best moved over this kind of terrain. It was a case of building stamina and lung power, and we did our best to copy his style and curb our competitive instincts. The barn was great as a first experience but almost immediately we discovered that by walking another mile or so to the edge of Loch Muick, we could have the greater freedom of Lochend bothy, for there we could have the benefit of a fire with an ample supply of wood from the adjacent stand of trees. This gave the advantage of year-round use for climbing and skiing. Lochend was a very basic building, being a simple, rectangular, wood-lined room, measuring around 30ft by 15ft, with a fireplace on one gable and the then standard two half doors as an entrance. It could accommodate a large number of climbers and became a popular base where lifelong friendships were made.

Without doubt, however, the most popular bothy by far was Bob Scott's bothy at Luibeg which was situated in Glen Derry and well placed for reaching the higher Cairngorms. The bothy was in a wooden outbuilding which stood a little back from Luibeg cottage where Bob, like generations of Derry keepers before him, lived. It was a cosy doss with a good fire; sadly, the building was burned down in the early 1980s and is no more. Bob had the roughest tongue of anyone I knew, which at first meeting could be very intimidating, but it was all just a front he put on as a way of making sure you had no doubt as to whose interests came first. So a conversation with Bob would usually go like this.

He would be in his usual position on a Saturday evening, hands deep in plus four pockets, leaning heavily against the open door of the bothy as we brewed up.

'Far are ye gyan the morn, lads?' He would ask innocently.

We would respond by saying something like, 'We were thinkin o' Corrie Etchachan.'

Bob: 'Fit!! Ye're bloody well nae. I'm shootin' hinds at the heid o' Derry on Monday. If I catch ony o' you buggers up there the morn scatterin' my beasts, I'll kick yer backsides a the wye doon tae Braemar! I think ye wid be better gyan on tae Macdui the morn.'

So, Macdui it was then.

If the Sunday happened to be a bad day, he would very often grab me. As an apprentice mechanic, I often had to repair a broken spring on his ancient 1934 Rover saloon but more often help in other ways.

Bob: 'Ye winnae be gyan on the hill the day.'

Me: 'Weel—'

Bob: 'That's fine, ye can gie me a han'.'

In his barn, he had a huge single cylinder diesel engine and I was useful in getting it started. To get it going, you had to pull a lever to decompress the cylinder, then with a crank you had to turn the engine as fast as you possibly could until there was sufficient speed, then throw the decompressor and this monster would slowly come to life. I can still hear the slow thump, thump, thump as it reluctantly got into its stride. Its purpose was to drive a fearsome circular saw which was outside and connected to the engine by a large belt connected to it through a hole in the wall of the barn.

Bob would find gigantic Scots Pine branches in Glen Derry, blown down in some gale and use his horse to drag them down to Luibeg. They were still too big to lift on to the saw bench and Bob would produce a two man saw of which I had very little knowledge. In my efforts to keep up, I would inadvertently push instead of pull and lock the saw in the cut.

'Dinnae push, jist pull ye daft bugger!' he would shout as I struggled to keep up with him

Being on the other end of the log as he pushed it into the circular saw was even more worrying. You could hear the whine of the saw slowing and the engine labouring as Bob enthusiastically fed the log in until I was aching to pull it back. But only at the very last moment would he allow the engine and saw a little respite.

Bob was unwittingly the person who helped to shape my future life. I remember clearly one morning just as I was setting out to the hill, we met at the edge of the Derry wood.

'Hiv ye ever seen a capercailzie nest?' he asked.

I hadn't the faintest idea of what a capercailzie was. At that age I was only interested on rock to climb or snow to ski on. So I had to say, 'No.'

He then led me to the edge of the wood and pointed to the base of a Scots Pine.

'There can ye see it?'

I could see nothing and Bob, seeing my mystification said, 'Are ye blin' man? There jist at the bottom of the trunk.'

I could still see nothing. So in exasperation, Bob, who named a succession of Jack Russell terriers Freuchan, called to the dog and sent it forward a few paces then called it back.

'There now can ye see it?'

At last I had detected a small movement and once my eye was in, I could see this huge bird sitting motionless until the dog forced a slight movement. I thought it was absolutely marvellous that such a large bird could merge so completely into the background to protect its nest. This was the beginning of an interest in wildlife which eventually enabled me to leave the restrictions of an urban engineering life to one where I was free to build a business based on the outdoors and which kept me in employment until I retired.

Despite the rough exterior Scott presented to the world, he had a tremendous sense of humour and an infectious laugh, with marvellous stories to tell; we all loved him. Stories about Bob, and Bob's own stories, are legion. Here a couple will have to suffice.

One of Bob Scott's tales was of a very early incident from his custodianship. It must have been about 1950 or earlier. There were very few people on the hills around Derry at that time and these two lads appeared who were hoping to get on to Braeriach and had a word or two with Bob on the way past. Some hours later one returned in an exhausted state to say his friend had collapsed somewhere between Corrour and Braeriach and that he had to come back for help. There was no mountain rescue in these very early days so Bob had to take the horse and trap down to Inverey, the location of the nearest phone, to contact the doctor in Braemar. He then gathered some of the other keepers and came back to Derry where there was one of those bamboo stretchers and they made their way into the Lairig, found the chap, strapped him into the stretcher and carried the unconscious man down to Derry – not an easy task. By this time the doctor had arrived.

According to Bob's account, they released the man from the stretcher and instead of the doctor immediately doing some resuscitation, he rifled through his pockets and brought out what to Bob looked like a packet of sweets. He popped one of these into the man's mouth and within minutes, the man was on his feet again. When Bob told a story like this his voice always rose an octave in mock indignation. 'If I kent a' I hid tae dae wis ti' pit a sweetie in his moo', the bugger wid hiv bin able to walk aff the hill himsel', athoot needin carriet.'

It seems the man was a diabetic and had gone into a coma with the exertion of going uphill and the companion was unaware of his medical condition.

Another story involved ourselves. It must have been a holiday weekend and we had ended up camping at the Derry wood, and having more or less run out of food on the Monday. I think all we had left was a tin of stew between four of us. We desperately needed something else to eke it out.

Bob at that time had a tattie patch near where we were camping surrounded by a high deer fence.

We looked longingly at this. There was no sign of Bob, so while the others kept watch, one of us nipped in, pulled out a few tatties from the middle of the row so it wouldn't be noticed and started boiling them up along with the stew. To our horror we heard Bob whistling as he left the house and crossed the long bridge over the Lui Burn and headed straight for us.

'Fit like, lads?' he said cheerfully.

We all tried to look laid back and casual but inside we were all uptight. We knew what was coming if he discovered what we had been up to. He then looked at the tatties and stew bubbling away in the dixies on the primus and said, 'Tatties and stew the day, is it?'

'Aye,' we said, trying to look unconcerned at the question.

Desperate to find some distraction, someone blurted out, 'We were in the Dubh Glen jist now and we saw a few deer carcases. Will ye hae tae beerie them?'

Thankfully, that did the trick. Bob's interest was now taken up by an extra duty he would have to take care of and he asked directions as to where the dead deer were lying and off he went again, already thinking of the next day's task. Immediately he was out of sight, we all heaved a great sigh of relief for we had just escaped a real tongue lashing.

Some of his tales were greatly humorous, and possibly a little tall. Bob was no respecter of persons – whatever their rank – and one day he entertained us with a tale of one of the 'toffs' who had recently visited the estate. As far as I recall, these were roughly his words.

'This mannie could hardly climb oot o' his bed in the morning nivver mind ging up a hill. He wis blin as a bat. I hid tae pit the barrel o' the gun aginst the stag and tell him tae pull the trigger. If I hidnae daen that I wid hae tae chase the puir wounded beastie a' o'er the Cairngorms till I got a clear shot. I hope tae hell he disnae come back. Min you, I dinna think he'll last another year himsel'.'

It's hard to estimate how many climbers from Aberdeen and sur-roundings there were in the early 1950s. As most of us worked on a Saturday morning, it was usual for us all to arrive in Bon-Accord Square to catch the 3.15pm bus to upper Deeside. There were usually two buses, one to Ballater, useful for Lochnagar and one to Braemar for the higher Cairngorms and the climbers would fill the back-end of each bus so that would amount to something like 50 at the very most. Travelling by bus and using the same bothies, we got to know each other very well and depending on where you hoped to go that particular weekend, you would join up with anyone who had the same climbing destination in mind. So the make-up of various groups would ebb and flow depending upon the interests of the various individuals at the time.

One of our group was George MacLeod, who would later go to the Antarctic, but at this time he had found himself a job with the Atholl estates as a forester. He would spend the week at Blair Atholl and come home every fourth week or so, bringing with him some interesting intelligence. He told us of the Tarf bothy, lying in an off-shoot of Glen Tilt and how it had more or less been aban-doned with most of its furnishings left intact. We had to see this! The details of the timing of the walk in are still a little hazy in my mind but it must have been a holiday weekend when we had more time because I am sure we spent the first night at the Bynack stables which lay about 12 miles west of Braemar, near the entrance to Glen Tilt. Bynack was still in a reasonable state at that time. There was at least one good, habitable, wood-lined room though the other parts were beginning to deteriorate quite badly. Now I believe it is pretty ruinous.

Next morning, we set off up the Bynack Burn and keeping An Sgarsoch on our right, passed over the hill and made our way up the Tarf Water. George hadn't exaggerated. The bothy was still fully furnished. There was a beautiful large, round mahogany table with a few chairs and a large dresser containing a full set of crockery. Jim Robertson had carried a large potted head all the way from Aberdeen and he now placed this on an elaborate ashet and we each spooned off a piece on to a matching plate. Bothying at its best. But I have to say, it was a creepy place at night.

Another foray into this area was during a September holiday weekend. We wanted to cover a large triangle by walking the old drovers' route over the Minigaig Pass. This entailed walking through the Tilt, crossing the Minigaig into Feshie, then returning through the Geldie. Something of a marathon in three days fully laden but with George's intelligence it was just possible. He knew of a bothy at the southern end of the Tilt which we could use.

For some reason I cannot now remember, the first day's walk involved us travelling the southern end of the Tilt in complete darkness. We relied on George's knowledge to find Gilbert's bothy. To this day I have no clear idea of where it was, as I can no longer find it, though I assume it was near Gilbert's bridge, but I can still remember every bump in its cobbled floor. The next day we set off very early, on across the top of the Bruar Falls and connecting with the Minigaig, thereafter over the high pass and down into the bothy of Ruigh-aiteachain in the Feshie. We knew this bothy very well for we used it at least once every year. It was our habit to spend our annual week's holiday, climbing somewhere in Skye or the North West and we would start the week by walking through the Feshie and finish the week by returning through the Lairig Ghru or vice versa.

Ruigh-aiteachain was in a very bad state then. The army had been using it as a training ground during the war and anything of any value had long since disappeared. At that time, it consisted of one barely habitable room with a door which was jammed shut. The only entrance was through what had been the window and at night a sheet of corrugated iron was placed over the gap to stop the rain and wind coming in. (My wife and I made a nostalgic visit to Ruigh-aiteachain a couple of years ago and were amazed at the transformation, after several years of maintenance by the Mountain Bothies association. It's now quite palatial by comparison, though the familiar bothy smell of wood-smoke, wet socks and cooking brought pleasant memories flooding back.)

On our September walk all those years ago, we completed our triangle by walking back to Braemar via the Geldie. It's a glen we were not enamoured with. It had a bothy, Ruigh nan Clach but we could find no reason to stay there. The Geldie was one of those places which you had to pass through in order to get to the Feshie or the Tilt and the bothy could be useful as a fall back if something went wrong, but the glen wasn't particularly attractive. There was, however one encounter there which I now regret. We were headed one dark night for Bynack, probably with the ultimate aim of going into the Tilt. Somewhere between White Bridge and Ruigh nan Clach, we heard the slow clip clop of hooves and out of the gloom emerged this figure, leading a pony with a stag carcase across its back. The man was very surprised to meet five shadowy figures moving towards him and said very curtly, 'Where the hell are you going?'

We had learned never to be too specific and simply replied, 'Oh, towards the Tilt.'

At this he lost his temper and said, 'You're bloody well not! You will turn round and get back to where you came from!'

There then began a real ding dong of an argument back and forth. He saying we had no right to be there and we saying we had every right. Finally, one of our group said, 'Where does your jurisdiction end?'

I think he then said, 'Bynack.'

So we said, 'That's OK then, we are passing through into the Tilt and you can't stop us.' With that he had to admit defeat and he disappeared into the darkness again.

Thinking back with 60-odd years of experience and a little more knowledge, I regret how that argument went, for now I have a lot more sympathy with the man's situation. This poor chap had probably spent a long day on the hill with his 'Gent Mannies'. They had shot a stag. The 'Gent Mannies' had gone back to the lodge for a bath and a jolly good dinner while he had come down the hill for the pony, gone up the hill again, humped the stag on to its back and this was him now at about 10.00pm at night just getting back. That was bad enough but he now had the prospect of five young climbers possibly scattering the deer during the weekend and he would have to find them again for another stalk on the Monday. So, it's a matter of give and take and a mutual respect for the other man's point of view, made a little easier over the last few years with better legislation.

We would use the bothy in Glen Gelder on occasion for it gave good access on to Lochnagar from the north side but it presented a few problems, being on the Queen's estate at Balmoral. Walking up Glen Gelder involved passing the keeper's house which at that time was occupied by a chap called MacHardy. I never personally met this fellow but his reputation preceded him. He was evidently built like a barn door and could be very intimidating – all the climbers had a healthy respect for him. So generally we used the Gelder bothy at the times of year when it was dark on arrival at Crathie. I remember that we carried a small can of oil, for there was a gate just below the house, and the gate squeaked as you passed through it. A touch of oil made it easier to sneak by the house without disturbing its occupant. As I remember, the bothy was well appointed, but when the political and terrorist problems arose in Cyprus during the middle '50s, security on that side of the hill became so tight that we decided it wasn't worth the risk.

However, the fact that we never met MacHardy meant that our stealthy tactics had been quite successful. Gelder was a base for the cliffs of Lochnagar, which were developed for climbing earlier than other Cairngorm mountains, and we did the classic routes, like Gargoyle, the Stack and – a favourite – Eagle Ridge. Our group were competent 'middle-grade' climbers, and though we enjoyed the classics, we left finding new routes to others.

As mentioned earlier, we used Corrour bothy at least once a year, starting out or returning from our annual week's holiday. Normally, it was easier and more comfortable for us to use Luibeg as a base at weekends and walk into the higher hills from there. My first visit to Corrour is a little hazy now but I seem to remember it still had a wooden roof and door with an earthen floor. There was a tiny fireplace but of course nothing to burn. There were tales that all you had to do was go outside, dig up a tree root from the days of the old Caledonian Forest and it would keep you warm all night but we were never successful in doing this for they were always sodden and wouldn't catch alight. The best we could do was burn heather and its roots but that didn't last more than a few minutes so it was usually a case of sitting in a sleeping bag on a pile of dry heather with all primus stoves going full blast to keep warm. I am not quite sure of the timing of this but sometime between 1950 and 1953, a few desperate people had used the door and part of the roof as firewood and around 1953, one of the armed forces had put on a metal roof, door and bench which ensured it could still provide shelter.

Access to the bothy across the Dee was still by rope bridge and the two ropes, one for the feet and one for the hands were by this time very badly stretched and sagging. With a heavy rucksack it required a special crossing technique. As soon as you were on the ropes, you had to push all your weight forward so that your body was at about 45 degrees to the water. This ensured that the weight of the rucksack was pushing you on to the upper rope rather than pulling you off. Of course it was quite a game when one person was halfway across for the others to try to pull the top rope over so that the unfortunate person was hanging the wrong way and the rucksack threatening to pull him into the water. It required almost superhuman strength to get to the other side without getting wet.

One could never be sure if the various estates had a policy of just allowing bothies to simply disintegrate or whether some estates actively pulled them down. I suspect Auchelie in Glen Ey was deliberately demolished, for while we were using it in the 1950s it was in really good order. Auchelie (we always pronounced it Acheeree) was one of the best bothies around the Eastern Cairngorms at this time. We used it more in winter than summer as a base for skiing, for the slopes around were ideal when the snow cover was good. Its main drawback being it was not quite in the right place for the higher hills, but it had excellent amenities. There were four rooms, the two downstairs were used mostly. One room had a good fireplace which we used for cooking and the other room for sleeping. The walls were woodlined as usual but the bedroom had the added refinement of a box bed with shutters which one could close to keep out the draughts. The other two upstairs rooms were mostly used at New Year when there was usually an overflow of climbers.

Having gone to live in the North West Highlands in 1963, it was some time before I revisited Glen Ey and a perfectly good building was no more. This may have been because the easiest way to remove the presence of climbers, hillwalkers and skiers was to deny them a base. This war against access was even more pronounced in the early '50s where we were met by active hostility in many quarters by landowners who were determined to keep us out. Much of our time was spent arguing with various characters. But over a period of many years, the arguments began to fade. The large landowners began to realise they were fighting a losing battle. We happened to be the vanguard of a movement which was gathering strength over the years and now it's difficult to imagine how anyone could deny access to any part of our mountains.

The Mountain Bothy Association probably came into being

just in the nick of time. Without their presence, most of the bothies would have disappeared long since and the climbing and walking experience of later generations would be so much the poorer. But not all Bothy Nights were spent in disused and abandoned former habitations, the ingenuity of the climbing fraternity often led to the construction of ad hoc accommodation, and none was more palatial and has been as long lasting as the Secret Howff of Beinn a' Bhuird, the true story of which forms the subject of my next chapter.

CHAPTER TWO

Building the Secret Howff
on Beinn a' Bhuird

BEINN A' BHUIRD and its environs was a favourite area for us. The Beinn had good corries for climbing in summer and skiing in winter, but it lacked a vital feature – a bothy. There had been one at the upper neck of the Slugain but evidently it had burned down in the 1940s and was now just a shell. One week in the late summer of 1951 we had been camping in the Fairy Glen in the Slugain and had decided for a change to walk down the Quoich on the Sunday. If I remember correctly, there were six of us in the group at this time: Jim Robertson, a stone mason; Charlie Smith, a diver with the Harbour Board; Doug Mollison who worked in the Town House; Jack Doverty, a steel erector; Jack Innes, a dental mechanic; and myself. We noted that the estate had been carrying out some forestry operation in the lower part of Glen Quoich. They must have been using a portable circular saw to square off logs as there were lengthy off-cuts lying all around. This planted the idea of us building a howff. Between us, we had all the manual expertise to build one very quickly from the materials lying around.

It took us only two weekends to carry in all the necessary tools to build a structure large enough to accommodate the six of us. The howff was built off the beaten track which went up Glen Quoich, and attached to an old Scots Pine for stability, had a sloping roof covered by part of a tarpaulin and coated with creosote to shed the rain and the other part of the old tarpaulin served as a door. It was ideal. The only drawback was the smell of creosote lingered with us for weeks on end but we had fond ideas of leaving our skis and winter gear there in the coming winter to save us the effort of humping them in every weekend. However these best laid schemes were many of such to 'gang agley', and the attempt of one of our member to get to our new doss almost led to disaster.

We were all very envious of Charlie Smith, who was a shipwright but had landed the job of the Aberdeen Harbour diver, in the days of steel helmets and lead boots. It meant he worked a five-day week and could leave for the hills on the Friday night late bus. On this particular weekend he shared the journey with a group of girls who were keen hill walkers and whom we knew well.

They were always frighteningly well organised. While we were living in squalor and eating out of tins, these girls would be sitting down to gourmet meals.

Charlie left the girls in Braemar and started the walk up the Linn o' Dee road, making for our new howff. Though there was no snow on the ground, it was a clear night with a very hard frost. On a few previous weekends, we had shortened the walk into the Quoich by fording the Dee. We had discovered a sandbar upstream of where the river Quoich joined the Dee and it was reasonably easy to cross at this point when the water was low. We had never attempted the crossing in the dark, preferring to walk as far as the Mar Lodge bridge and then sneaking across quietly to avoid disturbing anyone in the lodge opposite the bridge.

Charlie had just put in a hard day's work and didn't fancy the longer walk in, so thought he would attempt our fording point. He sat on the bank, took off his trousers and socks and tied them to the top of the rucksack, then putting his boots back on, he waded into the Dee and with the aid of a torch, tried to find the sandbar. He was quite successful on the first part but found the water coming up higher than he expected and then with one more step, he floundered and he was off his feet and floating downstream.

Always a very strong swimmer, Charlie threw off his rucksack and struck out for the bank he had just left, climbed out of the water and went in search of his rucksack, which luckily for him, had floated into the same bank a little downstream. He was now in very deep trouble. Everything he possessed was sodden, with no way of starting a fire since his matches were in the rucksack. With the hard frost already biting, he had to think quickly. There was only one thing for it. He had to walk as quickly as he could to Auchelie in Glen Ey about five or six miles away.

He climbed back up on to the Linn o' Dee road and was walking at high speed, minus his trousers. Meanwhile back in Braemar, the girls had just finished a leisurely meal at the Bruachdryne, a tearoom in the centre of the village which produced high teas at a very reasonable price and which was very popular with the climbing fraternity, and were boarding their taxi, for they too were making for Auchelie. As the car headed for Inverey, the headlights picked out a shadowy figure, hurrying along by the side of the road. Not recognising Charlie, they commented on how silly it was for someone to be walking in shorts at this time of the year.

The girls were already well ensconced in the bothy when the door burst open and this half-naked, bedraggled figure stumbled through the door. After the first initial shock, the girls' mothering instincts snapped into action and before he knew where he was, Charlie was sitting, wrapped in a warm, dry sleeping bag, in front of a roaring fire, with a steaming mug of tea in his hand while the girls dried out his meagre clothing.

Next morning, Charlie strolled down Glen Ey and crossed the Dee in a safer manner via the Canadian Bridge, which the lumberjacks had built during the war just upstream from Inverey in order to extract the timber from the Mar Estate. That evening in the Howff, we listened incredulously to his story and vowed never ever to attempt a crossing of the Dee in winter. However, the situation did not arise, for the next week, the estate discovered our hideaway and pulled it down. Our presence was never really welcome in the early 1950s. In retrospect, perhaps Bob Scott had probably found the right balance between climber and estate. He made a point of knowing everyone who came up to Derry regularly and with a foot in both camps, he would make sure that we didn't get in the way of what he had to do for the estate, while giving us every opportunity to find an alternative place to climb.

We had been beaten on this occasion but were still bent on

having a permanent base somewhere in the Quoich/Slugain area. We pondered the problem of where exactly to build this howff. It had to be large enough to accommodate at least the four of us plus a little more for any additional bodies and equipment but most important of all, it had to be in a position where it was least likely to be discovered by anyone from the estate.

Though Charlie was older, Jim Robertson, at the ripe old age of 23 and the only one with building experience, was the natural leader in this quest for the right place. He was a stone mason, a very highly skilled trade, a trade of men who took great pride in their work. In the autumn we scoured the glen and its environs and studied how the keepers used it during the season. At last, Jim's experienced eye alighted on just the right place which would involve the least amount of building and with a little artistry in choice of building material from surrounding scree, it would merge into the background once it was constructed. We had agreed that it mustn't divert us from enjoying some skiing if the winter was good but if some weekends were indifferent, we would spend it doing some building work. So some basic tools and materials were brought in and left in strategic places to be used when the opportunity arose.

The back wall was in fact already in position, for it was part of a very small rock face. Doug, Charlie and I stood back reverentially while Jim studied this face with a practiced eye.

'Right,' he said. 'We've tae decide hoo high we want to build this but we hiv tae keep in mind hoo we afix the roof tae this face. So the deciding factor is far there need tae be cracks in the face intae which we can drive dookins.'

'Dookins?' we looked at each other.

'Fit's dookins. Ye see, ye are learning a' the time,' said Jim. 'Dookins is an Aiberdeen builder's term for the pieces o' wood driven in atween steenwork, in this case a rock face, in order tae place a batten alang the face through which you can nail it securely and form a straight line along the face. Ye can then attach a roof and hopefully makk it wattertight.' We all nodded sagely and followed instructions. The roof wouldn't be as high as we would have liked, but as Jim said, we had to make use of what was already there. By the time we allowed a slope on the roof for running off water it would be quite low at the door at the far end. This could be an advantage of course, for we did want it to be as unobtrusive as possible.

The next task was to build a wall at right angles to the rock face. Jim had already taken this wall's position into account for there was a small heathery bank at more or less right angles to the back wall. All we had to do was dig it into a vertical wall and line it with scree which lay nearby, taking care to slope each layer of stonework slightly downward towards the bank, again for water run-off.

As autumn turned to winter in 1952, so the weather deteriorated. We had been camping at the site and taking down the tents at the end of each weekend and stowing them in the heather. We didn't want standing tents to attract attention. This saved us the drudgery of carrying them up and down the glen every weekend. The downside was they never dried out properly and it was very uncomfortable climbing into a wet tent every Saturday night when we arrived, but it also acted as a spur to finish the building work as soon as possible and place a roof on top. When the snow arrived, we would forget about the building project and make for an existing bothy where we were much more comfortable, and spend the Sunday skiing in some of the high corries deeper into the Cairngorms. But all the time work on the howff continued.

The front wall was very important for if not built properly it would give away our position. We took the greatest of care to get this right and Jim was a hard taskmaster. We were very fortunate that the geology of the area was mainly mica schist which meant that when water found its way between layers of schist and froze, the expansion shattered the rock along well defined layers, thus forming natural building stone. There was no shortage of this right at hand. So once again we would be laying the stonework sloping slightly downwards for water run-off and Jim would inspect our work from a distance and say at various points, 'No, that line will hae tae be improved, it disnae follow the natural flow of the hill,' – and we would have to remove it and start again. Over that winter we found a great number of adders hibernating in the scree from which we chose our building materials.

We were now into the spring of 1953 and had reached roof height. The tents were in a bedraggled state by now and we were longing to get a roof on. Naturally, our secretive movements in the glen had aroused the curiosity of some of our climbing friends who eventually realised what we were up to and were asking us if they could help. Since the next stage would involve the transport of heavy and bulky roof parts past the estate houses in the lower part of the glen, we readily agreed that if they assisted in taking this in, they would be allowed to make use of the howff in the future.

We had a meeting mid-week in Aberdeen and decided on the next step. I had already secured a gigantic ancient lorry tarpaulin which we would use to temporarily cover the open space where the joists and corrugated iron roof were to be placed. This would allow several of us to actually stay overnight for the first time in the howff while we worked on placing the roof in position the next day. Jack Doverty, then a scaffolder, had already secured some cast off sheets of corrugated iron and some of the others had various long battens of good timber.

We all assembled on the Saturday in Bon-accord Square in time to catch the 3.15pm bus to Braemar with our various roof parts. Luckily for us, Sandy, the inspector in charge of Strachan's buses was a man who was very sympathetic to the climbing fraternity and was very accommodating in allowing us to use the boot to carry all these mysterious pieces of equipment. We climbed aboard confident that we had thought of everything. It was only when we arrived at Ballater that we realised we had one enormous flaw in our scheme. The time had changed the previous week to British Summer Time. We would arrive at the road-end into the glen while it was still light.

At that time, the Braemar bus had a lengthy stop in Ballater and we had time to discuss our predicament. Someone came up with a brilliant solution. What we would do is continue on this bus up as far as Inver where there is a small inn about four or five miles short of our destination. We would take all our equipment and materials off the bus here, have a quiet drink and wait for the last bus up from Aberdeen to Braemar in about three hours' time when it would be dark, load on our gear again and carry on with our usual plan.

We duly unloaded everything at Inver, leaving it at the roadside, and strolled across the road to the Inn. It was a tiny place at that time and the pub consisted of a room about the size of the average living room with a tiny hatch where you could order a drink. We were none of us great drinkers. When you climbed and skied on the eastern side of the Cairngorms back then, the long walk in ensured there was no time to waste in a pub. So there was a debate as to what we should drink. A disembodied voice from the other side of the hatch said, 'I've got some Coronation Ale.' This of course was the year of the coronation and I think it was Dryburgh the brewer who brought out a special ale for the occasion. We thought we would try that and it turned out to be delicious, so we settled down for the long wait for the next bus, each of us feeling it necessary to buy a round for the others. It was only when someone looked at their watch and said it was time to go and we all stood up that we felt the full effects of the ale as we went reeling out of the door into the inky blackness of the night.

While we stood there in the darkness waiting, someone said, 'I dinna think we should come aff the bus at Keiloch far we usually do. There may be somebody fae the estate houses on the last bus. If we get aff there, they will suspect we are up tae somethin. I think we should come aff at the main gates and wakk up the driveway a short distance then cross tae oor track.' This seemed a very sensible precaution. We didn't want to blow the whole scheme now that we had done most of the work. The bus approached out of the darkness and because of the short distance we would be travelling, the driver and conductress kindly allowed us to take everything inside the bus since there were only a few passengers. This was easier said than done. The entrance to the bus seemed much narrower than we remembered it as we humped and heaved the materials aboard. The one thing that simply refused to go through the door was my rucksack, for it had this enormous tarpaulin strapped to the top and whichever way we tried, it simply would not go through.

I can still see the conductress, helpless with laughter, sprawled across a seat, as she watched our antics. At last with one pushing from the outside and another pulling from the inside we finally got it through.

Then we went through the performance once more in reverse when we reached the gates. As the bus drew away we all stood there in total darkness and someone said, 'Fa's got the torch?'.

Yet another flaw. No one had a torch. But the biggest flaw of all was immediately ahead of us. In our befuddled state we had all completely forgotten that the Great Gale earlier in the year had brought down all the mature trees in the small wood clustered around the gates and we all, with our various loads, stumbled and climbed over fallen trunks and enveloping branches until we were totally disoriented and had lost contact with the others.

Jim and I found ourselves together and tried to stay in contact as we fought our way forward, but we appeared to be making little progress. 'Ach, this is hopeless. I think we should jist bed doon far we can find somewyse flat and get up fan it's light.' That sounded a good idea and I unstrapped the tarpaulin from my rucksack, opened it up enough for us both to lie on something dry, got into our sleeping bags and instantly fell asleep.

At first light I opened my eyes, sat up and looked around. We were just clear of the woods but directly in front of the big house. I shook Jim violently, 'We've got tae get oot o' here. Look far we are.' He looked blearily around, then his eyes widened when they alighted on the big house. We hastily gathered everything together and rushed off to try and find the others.

The first person we came across was Doug. He was fast asleep, flat on the ground with his rucksack still on his back but his legs were above him draped over the trunk of a fallen tree. He had obviously tried to cross this, had somehow fallen backwards and had instantly fallen asleep. All the others were in similar poses. There was a short period of scrambling as they tried to find the various pieces they had discarded as they fought their way through the tangle, then we were on our way again.

There was only one house now to pass and we crept silently by trying hard not to rattle the corrugated iron sheets. When we reached the howff some time later, Charlie, who, stopping work on a Friday, had been up there waiting for our arrival the previous night, was livid that he had missed such a night. It was our usual practice that when we reached the open part of the glen, we would flash a torch. Charlie would be awaiting our signal and he would flash back and put a dixie of water on the primus and the tea would be awaiting our arrival. In this case, in our usual well organised way, we had forgotten the torch, even if we had made it to the open part of the glen and he was sitting there wondering what had happened.

We kept a tight lid on Coronation Ale after this debacle and work proceeded apace until at last the howff was complete. We spent many happy times here climbing in the summer, skiing in the winter and, as far as we were aware, the estate didn't ever come across it. (Many years later, Ian Mitchell told me that the game-keepers at Invercauld did know about the howff by the 1960s but tolerated it, as they knew where the climbers were if there was any bother. When the estate finally found out about it is another matter...) I suppose skiing was our main passion at that time and though we did climb in the corries of Bhein a' Bhuird, we left the pioneering of new routes such as Trident and Hourglass Buttress in places like Coire na Ciche to folk like Freddy Malcom and 'Sticker' Thom. And we had other passions too...

How this came about I am not quite sure, but in a curious way we had all discovered the pleasures of Italian Opera separately before we came together as a group of climbing and skiing friends. Charlie was the most knowledgeable. He was also good with radios. As mentioned earlier, he would have a dixie of hot water bubbling on the primus awaiting our arrival. The usual sight which greeted us as we crawled through the door was Charlie sitting quietly with a pair of headphones on, clearly enjoying a broadcast. While we made tea, he would put the headphones in a large dixie, then we would all stretch out around it and listen to a weekly broadcast of a complete opera direct from La Scala Milan. Sixty years on, this does not seem remarkable, but back then it was something of a miracle. Charlie would have an aerial stretched all over the hillside and it was amazing for us to be sitting on a hillside in Scotland, listening to a live broadcast from Italy.

Over the next few years, as is the way in life, we had reached the age when we were meeting girls and our weekends became more sporadic. In 1957, Jim married Chrissie, who was one of those girls whose hill walking group were so well organised and who had helped Charlie when he had his winter swim. The year 1957 was also when Asian Flu hit Aberdeen. It seemed only peripheral to our lives but it was to have a devastating effect on our group. At the age of 27, Jim Robertson became a victim and died suddenly. We couldn't believe that this had happened. He was such a strong fellow and at that age we all thought we were immortal. He had only been married three months. It didn't seem right somehow. We couldn't begin to think how it must have been for Chrissie. Some time later, a group of us climbed to the top of Beinn a' Bhuird and scattered his ashes there.

There is no doubt that this event had a profound effect on all of us and how we would live from now on. Our philosophy had changed overnight. We had lived for the day but now we would have to think of how we would live from now on. Life had suddenly become much more fragile than we had ever imagined and this event instilled in us a determination that at some point we would escape the drudgery of a factory with only the weekends in the mountains to look forward to. Of the whole group, Jim was the one who was most aware of the inequalities of life and how we must all try and improve it.

Jim was quite a committed communist and self-educated

working man who, without the benefit of higher education, had read widely. In Tom Patey's *One Man's Mountains*, Jim gets a mention as being 'engrossed in Marx' on the bus out to Deeside. He would come out with phrases like 'dialectical materialism', which lost the rest of us immediately, but he was much more aware of social conditions than we were and strove to make us understand how unequal society was. We were well aware of that but could not see how we could change it.

A crucial part of his interest in Russia – the USSR at that time – was that he made sure that we attended every concert in the Music Hall where the Soviets would send over their best artists. I seem to recall that the Red Army choir was one such. But the one I remember most was a group from Uzbekistan whose only musical instruments were tambourines tuned to tenor, baritone and bass. Their volume amazed me and the dancing group which they accompanied were very colourful and whirled around the restricted space of stage... So the howff of a Saturday evening could involve an Italian opera, a discussion on the problems of our society and a debate on the merits of the last Russian concert. When Jim died it left a gap in our conversation – and our lives. We were each now determined in our own way to do our utmost to change our lives for the better.

With Jim's passing – and the passing of time – our group whittled down and we used the howff less and less. Charlie, always a bit of a loner, continued to use the place and this led to it getting the later name of 'Charlie's Howff', mentioned in Tom Patey's *One Man's Mountains*. Only many years later was I to find out that the Secret Howff continued to give generations of mountaineers the pleasure it had given to its group of founder-builders.

CHAPTER THREE

Unsung Ski Mountaineering Pioneers

APART FROM bothying and mountaineering, our other great passion was skiing. Skiing in Scotland in the late 1940s and early 1950s was rather different to what we know today. The Scandinavians had been skiing in some form for more than 1,000 years, while the Alpine countries had been fast catching up since the 1920s. However, in Scotland only the middle classes could afford the pleasure and luxury of skiing, the equipment being so expensive, and since there was no form of uplift in this country, they travelled abroad. This all began to change after the Second World War. Large quantities of equipment produced in preparation for winter warfare now came on to the open market – the chief buyer in bulk being Millets Stores. It was now possible for the working class to buy an excellent rubber-lined frame rucksack for about 2/6p (25p), an ice axe of variable quality for about the same and a pair of skis for about £2.10 (£2.50). Of course, as an apprentice mechanic I was earning something like £1.8.6 per week, (less than £1.50), so it was in effect, two weeks' wages. Nevertheless, skiing was within reach.

A few of the young lads in Aberdeen who were attracted to the hills saw the possibilities, and like many others I bought my first pair of ex-army skis in readiness for the 1949/50 season. We soon discovered they were very basic. At that time, the correct length of ski for your height was for the upright ski to reach the palm of your hand held vertically above your head. Made from one piece of rather inferior wood, they had no steel edges and had a simple toe plate onto which was hooked a leather binding, which slipped around the heel of the boot. The result was that the heel was allowed to move up and down when walking in cross country but this was useless for any kind of turn. The boot would make the turning movement, slip off the edge of the ski and the ski would continue its forward straight line. We quickly discovered a step turn was the only way to change direction.

Since the quality of the wood was very poor, we had problems with the tip either breaking or simply flattening out over a period of time until there was very little upturn. Every so often we would spend an evening during the week when the tips were dipped in a bucket of boiling water. We would then jam them in a door, which a second man would hold securely while you slowly pulled the ski round to restore a deeply rounded tip. And yes, we know now that it should have been steamed but we had neither the knowledge nor the time then to make a steamer. With this rough-handed treatment, in heavy wet snow the tip would break eventually under pressure. Despite these drawbacks, we were off.

Kandahar bindings came in, as I recall, during our second season and were a vast improvement. These incorporated a flexible steel cable with a large wound spring at the heel. You could tension these with a clip in front of the toe plate and the heel was held tight by the cable, which was clipped to the side of the ski for downhill and was unhooked to allow the heel to rise for climbing and cross country. With this development we were able to move on to the more advanced turns. There was no one to teach us so it all had to be done by studying book descriptions and illustration. The perfect nursery slopes for us were in Glen Ey. (As mentioned earlier, there was an excellent bothy there named Auchelie. In good snow cover the bothy provided the perfect base with good gentle slopes close by.)

That Hogmanay of 1951 saw five of us – Jim Robertson, Charlie Smith, Doug Mollison, Johnny Vigroe and myself – sharing a very large Austin taxi in Braemar into which we piled all the rucksacks and skis. We were then transported up a very dodgy Linn o' Dee road which was under deep snow to Inverey where we immediately donned our skis, still without steel edges but with the new Kandahar bindings in the cross country position for the three-mile trek up to the bothy. It was a beautiful moonlight night and the recent blizzard had obliterated all evidence of the track, so we were choosing our own line. We each had the mandatory bottle of whisky in our rucksack, so we were moving fairly carefully, but even so the moonlit slopes were difficult to read and Charlie Smith went down with a great clatter. We all laughed of course, but then he said, 'There's something weet rinning doon my leg. Oh no, I hope it's blood, nae the whisky.' It wasn't blood. A precious bottle had been lost.

At that time, most people worked on Christmas day but had three working days holiday at the New Year. So we had time to concentrate on getting the stem turns and stem christies right by watching each other and deciding where and when the weight should be at a particular place on the turn. The result was that each one of us developed a unique style which the rest of us could identify from miles away for years to come. By the third day we had developed a confidence which was probably unjustified by our actual capabilities and decided we were ready for our first ski mountaineering trip. The plan was to climb Creag an Lochain to the south of Auchelie and follow the ridge along to Carn Creagach. Both hills were just under 3,000ft, which we thought we could cope with. This would leave us with a nice downhill run to Altanour lodge, which was even then a broken down bothy at the head of Glen Ey. We would then return to our base along the floor of the glen.

We hadn't reckoned on the weather changing. This was in the days before transistors made it possible to carry a small radio for forecasts. We just had to take whatever came along. And come along it certainly did. By the time we had reached the top of Creag an Lochain, the wind was screaming from the North East and then the snow hit us almost as a solid wall. There have only been a handful of times in my lifetime on the hills when I have experienced a blizzard of this magnitude. Any communication between us was impossible because of flapping cagoule hoods and howling wind. Soon it became very difficult to remain in visual contact with the others and we just plodded along in our own little world. Eventually, just ahead of us we could just make out something of a greenish, blue colour. A few more steps and we all came to a halt on the edge of an icefield, which sloped at an alarming angle down to our right.

Though we couldn't communicate, we individually realised the wind had pushed us off the crest of the ridge and into the headwall of the burn, which comes off Carn Creagach and which earlier freeze and thaw conditions had converted to solid ice. This was beyond our skiing experience. The question was how to cross it. We still did not have steel edges on our skis, so were unsure whether we could get a grip with our, by now slightly rounded, edges. Should we attempt to cross it on ski, take our skis off, or perhaps turn directly into the wind and driving snow to regain the ridge? This alternative, though practical, was not appealing. We each stood there deliberating using our sticks to brace ourselves against the wind which threatened to drive us on to the ice. Doug Mollison made a decision. He bent down, took off his skis and we watched as he slung them over his shoulder and edged on to the ice. Almost immediately the wind caught him, spun him round and he was off at high speed down the steep gully and out of our sight. We each stood there in silence, our slowing brains taking in the situation. We knew he would not come to real harm. There were no outcrops of any kind. He would have to find his own way back.

We now knew not to take the skis off and that we had to regain the ridge. So we backed away from the ice and reluctantly turned into the wind and snow to climb on to the right side of the hill. By one of those freaks of nature, the driving snow parted momentarily as we came over the crest and we could see directly below us the trees of Altanour. Without hesitation we all pointed our skis downhill as the weather closed in again. This led to another new experience for us. We had lost contact with each other as we each had chosen our own line and were alone in a total whiteout with no point of reference. The result was the feeling at one point that you were progressing at a moderate speed, then you would hit something that threw you off balance and you would pitch into the snow and only then realise you had been going quite fast. At other times, you felt you were racing down, you would get scared, fall and realise you had hardly been moving. Finally and thankfully, we arrived at Altanour where conditions were much more moderate and we were able to discuss the situation. We were all concerned that we had left Doug to fend for himself, so we got back to Auchelie as fast as we possibly could, only to find Doug toasting himself at the fire. He had slid all the way down the gully, losing his skis on the way, and, now out of the worst of the weather, he deduced he was in the Connie Burn. So it was quick and easy for him to get back from there, though he spent the next weekend searching for – and eventually finding – his skis.

So ended the first lesson. We had learned how to control the skis but still had a lot to learn about reading the weather in winter, a vital factor which would only come by experience. In mitigation, our summer activities meant we had a reasonable knowledge of the terrain and we resolved to explore much further afield during the summer so that we could then rely on an inbuilt knowledge of the Eastern Cairngorms, which we could fall back on in winter.

Time, distance and transport were the major constraints in those days. Most of us worked on a Saturday morning; we had to use public transport and the winter days were short. So we would normally arrive in Braemar about 6.30pm on the Saturday night, and if there were enough of us and we could afford it, we took a taxi to the Derry gate. From there it was a four-mile walk or ski to Derry Lodge and Luibeg where Bob Scott, the keeper would let us use his bothy. The next day would be spent getting on to the snow, weather permitting, then the reluctant trudge back to Braemar to catch the 7.00pm bus to Aberdeen. One day from that period stands out. It was early spring and must have been one of those rare occasions when we were given a key for the Derry gate at a cost of 2/6p. This allowed us to take the taxi right up to Derry Lodge and for the vehicle to pick us up again the following day in just enough time to get back to Braemar for the bus. The Sunday turned out to be one of those days one dreams of but seldom gets in Scotland – cloudless blue sky, no wind and excellent snow cover on the high tops.

The snowline was about 2,000ft, so we carried the skis all the way up the Lui Burn and donned them on the Sron Riach. The aim was to take in Ben Macdui and see how the time went from there. So we contoured up the hill, the snow conditions getting better and better, and we arrived on the summit in remarkably good time. There was not a breath of wind and visibility was crystal clear. We debated our next move and someone suggested going across to look into the Cairn Lochan corries. That seemed a great idea, so we pushed on across the plateau. Only other mountain skiers would appreciate the tremendous pleasure of gliding along effortlessly on a high top in perfect conditions with good companions, each taking a turn to break the trail but taking their own individual line on the downhill stretches. In no time we were peering into Coire an Lochan and had to consider our route back. The natural line was to skirt the Feith Buidhe slabs at the head of Loch A'an then head down to the frozen Loch Etchachan. We were still reluctant to leave the snow by going down through Corrie Etchachan, so we contoured around the side of Derry Cairngorm and on to the Carn Crom ridge and finally ran out of snow halfway down Carn Crom. There was just enough time to collect our gear at Luibeg and meet the taxi at Derry Lodge. One of many memorable days.

Gleann an t-Slugain and Beinn a' Bhùird had always been a favoured area for us in summer. We would camp in the Fairy Glen at the head of Slugain and climb in the corries of the Beinn, go on to Ben Avon or wander down the Quoich. We had long noticed that the shallow corrie to the south of Coire na Ciche held good snow long after it had gone elsewhere. The difficulty was carrying skis and winter camping equipment to the head of the glen, apart from the discomfort of winter camping, and this did not appeal. This is where our new 'secret' howff repaid all our building efforts.

From this base we could explore the Beinn on ski. I think the earliest we skied there was the third week in October, though of course the early snow didn't last and had thawed by the following weekend. Almost invariably we ended the skiing season here on the third week in April for this was the Aberdeen Spring Holiday. What we had discovered on our various ski tours across the summit plateau was a wide curving gully (Alltan na Beinne) which left the top behind A' Chioch and swept south and down at just the right angle to finish in the Dubh Glen. It was the perfect end to a good day's skiing but a longer trek back to the howff, after we had finished the run. This took a bit of the edge off the experience, so we gave thought as to how we could end the run more satisfactorily.

We considered this and came up with a solution. Every Spring holiday we would take a taxi to the Derry gate, walk about one mile beyond the Black Bridge then cut through Clais Fhearnaig and into the Dubh Glen to camp. We each carried several bottles of beer (no cans then) which we resisted drinking and buried them in the snow wherever the Altan na Beinne run ended that particular year. Then the next few days, we would climb to the summit, explore the corries and take the last run of the day down the curving gully and plunge our hand into the snow at the end, to extract an ice cold beer. This seemed to us to be the ultimate in luxury.

We were all by 1955 earning a little more money and had learned a little more about the cradle of skiing in Norway. We had always hoped to get there so when the Norwegian Government and the Fred Olsen Line came up with a scheme to encourage tourism in their country we jumped at the opportunity. For a comparatively cheap price we could cross from Newcastle to Bergen and then on by train to a tiny hamlet called Ustaoset near Geilo where we were to be housed in a hostel for two weeks. The only part of this we were not keen on was the word hostel for we thought of this as being the soft option after a lifetime of bothying. However, the chance to be in Norway in March was too good to miss and we spent a long winter saving as much as we were able to cover the cost.

We were not disappointed. The price had included the hire of skis and an instructor if required. As we were the only group who had taken up the offer in the period, the young lad designated as instructor – seeing we were already fairly proficient – agreed to guide us on a number of ski mountaineering trips. The most enjoyable of these was a short trip by train up to the highest point of the trans-Norwegian railway at Finse at around 5,000ft. When we alighted at this station, there was no sign of the building. It was totally enveloped in snow with only the windows and exit cut through. We donned the skis immediately and started the climb into the Hallingskarvet mountains.

I remember it as a beautiful sunny day with just a slight breeze. We had taken nothing with us in the way of food, for our Norwegian friend said mysteriously that we could get something at the top. It was a long climb but we were already anticipating the downhill run, as it was an open area where we could make wide sweeping turns. Then, somewhere ahead of us, we could see some kind of building. This was Prestholtsetter, our destination. It was a revelation for here we were able to have a good meal. Everything was brought up from Finse by sledge to us. It was sheer luxury. We were used to the limiting factor of carrying everything with us we could possibly need. The downhill run back was beyond our dreams. As the only group on the mountain, it being mid-week, we were able to make full use of every inch of snow and swung wildly from one side of the mountain to the other until we were at the station entrance again. Even after 60 years it stands out in the mind as a truly memorable day.

The one thing that impressed us most were the Norwegian skis. They were light years ahead of anything we had experienced. We were still used to skis made out of a single piece of wood and without steel edges. Charlie possessed the best pair of these – his were made of a single piece of hickory, regarded as the best in those days. Their only drawback was the weight. Carrying them any distance caused Charlie to fall behind a bit.

Campbell's was a sports shop on Bridge Street in Aberdeen. It was the only place we could buy tricounis (nails) for our climbing boots. They covered all kinds of sports and, seeing there might be a market for skis, had a firm make skis for them. They were the first laminated ski I remember where the ski was made up of several layers of wood capped top and bottom by plastic. Crucially, they did not have a steel edge, which meant that for us they only lasted one or two seasons. So while in Norway, a visit to a ski shop in nearby Geilo was a must.

This was an eye opener. We were confronted by rows of skis from very narrow touring skis to the wide downhill variety – all with steel edges. They were agents for Greswig, which at the time was the leading ski manufacturer in Norway. The young lad who had the shop told us to try them for flexibility etc and we gingerly pushed and pulled the ski back and forth. He came across and said, 'No, no, you must push them hard,' and he proceeded to push and pull them in every direction. We had never seen a ski in Scotland bend to such a worrying degree. I immediately decided that I must have a pair whatever it cost. In fact it took everything I had left on me, but was worth every penny.

The only problem was that, on returning to Newcastle, the customs officer immediately confiscated them, since I had spent all my cash and had nothing left to pay the import duty. It's an indication of how we all trusted each other in those days that a young woman, who was a complete stranger, overhearing my problems immediately offered me the cash to pay the duty. It was a gesture for which I was very grateful and I repaid her as soon as I got home. I look at ski equipment now with envy. There are remarkable developments in skiing and sometimes I wish I were starting all over again. But we are all of our time. You can go up and down a crowded piste all day and be quite happy, but there is nothing like having a whole mountain to yourself where you are choosing your own line and working out how to use the hill for the maximum enjoyment.

At the time it did not really occur to us how pioneering our activities were, although we hardly noticed another skier in the eastern Cairngorms in the early 1950s. Occasionally, a lone skier would appear who would pick a downhill route and ski that one route all day, but we encountered no-one doing cross country stuff as we were. Indeed, it was only more than a half century later that I discovered, when I wrote an article for a skiing magazine, that my descent of the Black Spout on Lochnagar in 1956 had been its very first descent!

CHAPTER FOUR

Transport Problems
in the 1950s

BACK IN THE 1950s, getting to the mountains was more of a problem than it is today. Buses were irregular and very few people had cars or access to cars. We were still a fluid group of about eight, climbing and skiing together at weekends. The conversation was continually reverting to how good it would be if we had some kind of independent transport. However, the prospect of possessing a car seemed wildly beyond our means, until one of our group, who had a contact in Banchory, mentioned that someone was selling a huge 1934 Armstrong Siddeley; the long version, which could carry eight passengers. As the only member of the group serving an apprenticeship as a motor mechanic, and also possessing a driving licence, I was delegated to explore this possibility, and so three of us found ourselves one evening on the outskirts of Banchory looking round this huge vehicle. The Armstrong-Siddeley was a luxury car of the 1930s, which cost between £1,000 and £1,500 depending on the version; King George V owned one back then.

Though 20 years old, the bodywork was still in reasonable condition. The seats were real leather and the interior boasted polished wood. It had most probably been laid up during the war. Mechanically, it seemed fairly sound, but it was the sheer size that proved the most attractive aspect. It certainly was a monster. It had a spacious bench seat in front which could easily accommodate two people plus driver. From the back of this seat, two further 'dicky' (folding down) seats could be folded down facing rearwards and then there was another bench seat accommodating a further three people right at the back. A total of eight seats. It sounded too good to be true. The question was how much was the seller asking? After much haggling, we agreed on a price of £20 and the owner was to hold the price till we contacted the rest of the group.

Everyone was enthusiastic about the idea and each of us scraped around the next few days, managing to raise £2.10s each (£2.50). A few evenings later found us driving this monster of a car back to Aberdeen. It must be remembered there was no such thing as an MOT in those days, so we were not inhibited about how we loaded it. It had an outside rack on the rear end on to which we piled as many rucksacks as possible, the others being stored on the floor between the dicky and the rear seats. Skis were loaded on either side of the middle passenger on the rear seat and rested on the edge of the front seat between the two dicky seat passengers. Yes, it may have been uncomfortable for the others, but as it was only for a couple of hours drive to Braemar and beyond, and as I was the only driver, it didn't bother me too much. That was to come later. We were now free as birds to reach the upper reaches of the Cairngorms as soon as we were released from work and return when we saw fit...

Or so it seemed.

During the week, the car was parked in the garage where I worked and as we all (except Charlie) worked on a Saturday morning, I would take my weekend equipment into work with me on Saturday and at 12 noon would drive round picking up the others and then set off up Deeside.

This was the late autumn of 1954 and without the skis aboard, the first expeditions were the height of luxury. We would have a leisurely drive up to Braemar and along the Linn o' Dee road stopping to pick up the key for the gate on the Derry road at the gatehouse for Mar Lodge and be at Luibeg without expending any effort whatsoever. It meant that on the Sunday, we could delve much deeper into the farthest corries without the limiting factor of getting back for the 7.00pm bus from Braemar. The biggest drawback for me was that because the others knew that they could drive themselves hard on the Sunday in the knowledge that their day was finished as soon as they arrived back at Derry Lodge. I, on the other hand, had to do all the driving back to Aberdeen. So it was usually the case that immediately we were on the Linn o' Dee road, all the others fell fast asleep and there was complete silence all the way home until I dropped them off on their doorstep. But it seemed a small price to pay for this added freedom.

The car had an epicyclic gearbox and a fluid flywheel- state of the art at that time, and this made for the smoothest of gear changes, with a lovely whirring noise as accompaniment. However, the vehicle soon began to show some of its idiosyncrasies. The first was when we stopped at Coilacriech outside Ballater for petrol. The pump then was on a steep camber of the road and having filled up, the car refused to start again. After several attempts to start to no avail, it dawned on me that the angle of the car had something to do with it, so I allowed it to freewheel backwards on to the flatter part of the road and it then started promptly. Puzzled by this, I mentioned the problem to one of the oldest mechanics during the course of the next week.

'Ah,' he said. 'It's one of two things, or it could be both. The petrol pumps on these older cars were not very good and it has a Stromberg carburettor which means that sometimes if the angle is too great the pump can't deliver enough petrol to feed the tricky float chamber of the carburettor. It can only get worse. Eventually, you will come out some morning and keep spinning the engine with the starter motor until the battery runs down simply because the petrol pump is too weak to deliver the petrol to start the engine. You really need a new pump but you will be very lucky if you find one.'

'So what do you think I should do about it?' I said, knowing that there would be times when this could prove a problem.

'Let me have a think about that,' he said.

A few days later he came back and said, 'I think I've found a solution. I've made this little tank for you which holds about a pint of petrol and it's got a little tap on the bottom with a tube. What I want you to do is cut the petrol feed between the pump and the carburettor and put in a T junction so you can divert the petrol supply up to the little tank which you screw on to the bulkhead ABOVE the engine. Before you switch off the engine at the end of the run, you open this tap, and with the engine running, you divert some of the petrol up into the little tank. You can then switch off and in the morning open this tap, allowing the petrol to run down by gravity into the carburettor and it should start first thing.' I followed his instructions to the letter and it worked a dream. So one problem solved, but a few more to come. The winter of 1954/55 proved to be quite a severe one, much to our delight, and so the skis became a welcome additional load. In the early part of the winter, we decided that there may be good skiing if we drove up the Devil's Elbow road to Glen Cluny Lodge, which was derelict then and is now long since gone. Using this as our overnight base, we could climb the Baddoch Burn and get to the good snow high up on the hills between there and Glen Ey. This would only be possible if the lower reaches of the road from Braemar to the Elbow were reasonably clear of snow – for at that time there was no habitation beyond Auchallater, and the ploughs would not venture beyond this point. If there was some snow and a little drifting, then we hoped our weight and speed would usually see us through.

By mid-winter there were severe frosts and heavy snow and we thought it time we were back at Luibeg. On this particular weekend, there had been a heavy snowfall around Braemar and we were determined to reach Derry Lodge. We stopped at the Mar Lodge gatehouse for the key for the Derry gate and 'Flash Gordon'. (He came by this name because we all as children had seen the dreadful science fiction films about Flash Gordon, and this Gordon drove a motor bike with a side-car shaped like a torpedo or space ship. His nickname was inevitable.) He came to the door and said, 'You'll be very lucky if you get up there tonight.' But we were very confident that our weight and engine power would get us there.

With the gate open, even in the darkness we could see that the wind had been drifting the snow heavily across the track, and we debated our strategy. It was a long shallow climb up towards the Black Bridge over the Lui Water, but we knew because of the wind direction that our greatest challenge would be a few yards short of the bridge. At that time, there was a small area of dense forest on a turn of the road down to the bridge and we knew from past experience this was where the greatest drifting would be

It would be best if we could try to build speed as we climbed the gentle rise and increase it when we hit the flat piece of road before the wood. The first part went very well and we hit the flat part of road going full tilt. In the headlights I could see the drifted snow at the edge of the wood much higher than we ever expected and we hit the drift head on. The snow flew out over the windscreen and within a few yards we ground to a halt. So deep were we in, that we couldn't initially open the doors, but with a bit of shoving and pushing, we all managed to get out and survey the situation.

We were well and truly stuck and were paying the price of our over confidence. Fully prepared as ever, we had taken nothing with us to cope with such a situation and it was only through the use of the tail end of skis and hands to remove the excess of drifted snow, then muscle power and the car in reverse that we finally escaped the drift. We had to admit defeat; Luibeg was not going to be possible that night. It was now very late at night and we had to think of an alternative. No one was very keen to ski the remaining distance to Derry and even less keen to ski up Glen Eye to Auchelie.

Then someone came up with a great idea. There was an outhouse next door to an empty house called Claybokie (now re-named and gentrified) on the way to the Quoich and before Mar Lodge. We could all probably squeeze in there for the night and re-assess everything in the morning. Having all agreed on this, we spent some time in stamping down an area large enough to turn the car and drove back down to the Derry gate once more.

It should be explained that not many people kept cars on the road in the winter at this time and those who did had to put an antifreeze called Bluecol into the radiator. This was horrendously expensive back then. As an apprentice, I remember it being treated like liquid gold when a car had to be prepared for winter and it was measured out very exactly. Needless to say, the capacity of our radiator was such that there was no way we could afford such a luxury, so the car was drained when left overnight. We parked the car near the gate and I diligently drained the radiator. There was clearly going to be a severe frost that night. Donning our skis, we covered the short distance to Claybokie in no time and were ensconced, somewhat tightly, in the little wooden outhouse and after a brew up were soon all fast asleep.

Next morning, we awoke to find every sleeping bag frozen down the outside where our breath had condensed. When broken, eggs came out crystallised. We learned later that Braemar had broken its record for the lowest temperature recorded there, and it had got down to 44 degrees Fahrenheit of frost (-24.5 C). There was so much snow around we decided not to do anything desperately exhausting but to just do a little ski touring in the general area between the Quoich and the Lui Burn. After a great day and a half decent meal in our temporary shelter, we returned to the car as darkness was falling.

We now had to refill the radiator. I always made sure that we carried one of those collapsible buckets for this purpose. As those who know the area around the Derry gate are aware, the nearest water lies down a very steep drop to the Lui Burn. This did not seem much of a problem, for with eight of us, a bucket chain was easy. The burn was of course totally iced over and the first man had to break through the ice to fill the bucket. This was slowly passed up the line and I stood on top of the bumper to pour the water into the radiator. It was of course a laborious process which took some time but at last the radiator was full and we were ready to go. I primed the little tank with petrol as usual and with that the vehicle started first time which was a great relief. We had driven just a few yards when there was an almighty bang and I hastily stopped the engine. Warily, I lifted the bonnet. The problem was obvious. There must have been a little water left in the water pump the night before which had frozen, or possibly the water had been freezing as we poured it in to the radiator. Whatever the case, the flexible drive to the water pump had sheered and there was now no means of circulating the water round the cooling system and we were stuck.

I explained the problem to the others and we pondered a solution. After a lengthy discussion in which we all had some input we came up with something which we hoped might – or might not – work. As a rule of course, I always carried tools in the car and someone had a fish slice with lots of holes and slots. It was my job to take off the broken flexible drive while someone else, with the aid of a chisel, fashioned a rough replica out of the fish slice. By lining up the holes and slots with the two ends of the drive, we were able to insert two bolts which hopefully would get us home. Just to make sure there was no ice left in the system, we closed the bonnet, threw two sleeping bags over it and thrust two primus stoves under the engine. This car was so high off the ground there was no danger of anything catching alight. We then sat in the car for an hour getting out occasionally to check the engine and getting our own circulation going again.

At long last we decided it was safe to start the engine and fearfully watched as our Heath Robinson repair spun at the side of the engine. It seemed to be holding so we cautiously climbed aboard and drove slowly and carefully back to Aberdeen. The others, as usual, were fast asleep without a care in the world while I worried my way home. Never a keen mechanic, I was fast falling out of love with this form of transport. It was lucky that we were mostly blue collar workers who were used to finding a solution to practical problems but that is precisely what I wanted to get away from at weekends. And here I was having a busman's – or motor mechanic's! – holiday.

It was only a few weekends later that we had decided to do a little winter climbing for a change and as Lochnagar was one of our favourite venues, we drove up Glenmuick and parked the car in the little quarry at the road end, which was used for road fill, and walked the remaining distance to Lochend Bothy. Snow conditions were excellent and we had a great day in the corrie, finally coming off the hill as dusk was falling. After a brew up at Lochend we headed back to the car where we loaded up all the equipment and jumped in.

As soon as I pushed the starter button I knew we were in trouble. The engine turned over but only very slowly. It was immediately obvious the dynamo had not been charging the battery on the previous day. My memory is no longer good enough to remember why I hadn't noticed this at the time, but if there was a warning light, then the bulb was a dud or it may well have been there was no warning light – this being in the era before the sophistication of such things. Whatever the case, it was important to conserve what life there remained in the batteries. It was a case of everyone out and with seven pushing we succeeded in bump-starting the car without too much difficulty. It was a reasonably clear frosty night and I decided that we could manage down the Glen Muick road without the aid of lights. When we reached the main road at Ballater I switched on side lights. Traffic at this time was very, very light and we travelled carefully along the road optimistically hoping the batteries would last the distance to Aberdeen. It was a forlorn hope.

As we reached Dinnet, the engine began to spit and splutter for there was not a strong enough spark to ignite the petrol mixture. As we reached the outskirts of the village where there was a dense conifer wood (recently cut down), we struggled to pass a lone cyclist probably heading for the pub. What I hadn't realised was that the engine was misfiring so badly the unburned mixture was flooding into the exhaust, which by this time was very hot. Suddenly, there was a great explosion which lit up the entire woodland. The cyclist was so shocked that he fell off his machine and into the ditch. He was not best pleased as we apologised but accepted that it was not deliberate and mounting his bike again proceeded on his way.

Now what? We were well and truly stuck. There was the AA of

course, but membership of that was well outside our league. Then someone remembered the last bus to Ballater would be passing, going in the other direction, very shortly. We could at least get back there. Another possibility struck me. If we had time, I could take out the two six-volt batteries and take them with us, for I knew Strachan's bus garage in Ballater had a bay for charging batteries.

I was still feverishly trying to extract the batteries from under the seats when we could see the lights of the bus approaching. The others dashed to the other side of the road to flag it down and ask the driver if he could possibly wait till I removed the batteries. Even now I am still astonished at how relaxed, laid back and helpful these drivers were. He had only one or two passengers and was quite happy to wait till I finally succeeded in putting them aboard while the others loaded our equipment. In the short distance back to Ballater, I explained our predicament and asked permission to use their battery charger in the garage. He agreed quite readily and not only assisted me in wiring them up, but allowed us to sleep in the waiting room till he came back first thing on the Monday morning for the run to Aberdeen. Once again we boarded the bus and with the newly charged batteries back in place there was enough charge in daylight to get us home once more.

Needless to say our families were thinking that either we were lying at the foot of some snow climb or involved in an accident on the way home, there being no direct phone connection to our homes in those far off days. So we were getting a lot of stick at home and I was certainly coming round to the opinion that I was working harder at weekends than ever.

During the course of the next week, I removed the dynamo and, following the advice of the specialist in auto electrics at my work, managed to effect a repair, but had already decided that if there was another major problem, I would distance myself from the role of driver-mechanic. I did not have long to wait. It was only two weeks later as we were driving up Deeside that we hit a very deep pot-hole and broke a rear spring. This was not at all surprising since we were consistently overloading the vehicle. We all got out to survey the damage and I immediately said, 'Well, that's it. I am certainly NOT going to repair that.' To my surprise everyone agreed that they had had enough of this 'luxury transport' and we voted to get rid of it.

As it happened, we were quite near the Glen Gairn road-end with a telephone box quite close so I called up a lad I knew of called Willox, who owned the garage in Ballater. Would he be willing to come out with a breakdown vehicle and pick up the Armstrong Siddeley? I told him he could have it for nothing if he wanted to use it for spares. To our surprise he readily agreed and I then wished we had asked him for £20 to recoup our losses. But to be fair, we had had a great winter's use out of it and despite several mishaps, we had in the main come out of it very well. Or so I thought till I recently did an internet search and found that a model very like the one we had back then was now selling as a vintage car... for £20,000!

Maybe we should have held onto it after all...

For me, the real luxury after a hard day on the hill was getting aboard a Strachan's bus knowing that whatever happened it was someone else's problem, so I was glad to see the back of the beast. The winter of 1954/5 turned out to be a very cold one and my chief memory is of severe frosts on hard snow, where the deer could not dig their way through to the vegetation beneath. The banks of the upper part of the Dee were lined with deer carcases in the spring. Luckily, having got rid of the Armstrong Siddeley, I felt more confident that none of those corpses would be ours, though I was still chained to other machines at work...

CHAPTER FIVE

Breaking Out: Choosing a Life in the Highlands

FROM MY position by the factory window, I could look beyond the hated machinery to a fairly primitive machine built long before the turn of the century. It was never used now and kept more as a curiosity than for any positive purpose. My father had told me that my grandmother had operated this very machine when it was new. It was an odd feeling to look at the worn board where the envelopes were kicked out and think of my grandmother's busy movements sorting them into the bundles of 25 which had created those hollows. I had never known her. How had she felt as a young girl sitting in front of this machine? Did the strict disciplinarian attitudes of the time allow her to have thoughts of revolt such as I was experiencing? Were we here simply to serve the industrial machine or did we have a freedom of choice? At this time, the only choice seemed to be to be working or to be unemployed. If you were working, you were fortunate. Liking or disliking the work did not come into the equation. No one could afford the luxury of a philosophy. It didn't pay to think too deeply; it only depressed one more.

There was no way I fitted into factory life. I knew nothing of football or cared about the latest gossip on the factory floor and while I applauded the efforts of the trade union to improve working conditions, the politics, intrigue and rules bored me to death. An aversion to any kind of authoritarianism or bureaucracy had been ingrained in me by my mountaineering friends. We had gone out of our way to avoid belonging to any club or organisation. Our thinking at the time being that where there are organisations, there are rules and we were in the hills to escape these. Bureaucrats seemed intent on trapping us into conforming to a specific pattern of behaviour and eventually we become incapable of believing any alternative is possible. Here I was, 28 years of age, and still hadn't found a way of life which was bearable. Material success was of no interest to me. What I needed was a way of life which was not alien to my nature. A life which was fulfilling in a way that was evident to me each weekend. Achieving it appeared to be utterly beyond my reach.

What I hadn't realised was that some 500 miles to the south, Derek, my brother in law, was experiencing much the same disenchantment with his life. He had married my wife Norma's sister, Helen and worked in the aero design section of Rolls Royce in Derby. He too was an outdoors man at heart and a good naturalist. In the summer he would come up with his young family and spend a few days with me in the Cairngorms where we discovered we had a great deal in common. We would roam the hills and have flights of fancy where we imagined doing this for the rest of our lives. We each realised that the other would be happier in another occupation.

It was one day early in the summer of 1963 that I arrived home late because of a machinery breakdown to find a letter from Derek awaiting me. We did not normally have much contact apart from his summer visits so it was with some surprise and interest that I opened it. He had heard that Ford were to bring out a new type of vehicle called a minibus which would be capable of taking 11 passengers. Could this possibly be our way out? At last, a glimmer of light at the end of the tunnel.

A flurry of letters were exchanged as the ideas began to form. If we each had one of these buses, we could bring each other up to speed in our particular strengths and take a group apiece into very remote areas by minibus, then explore on foot the places difficult to reach in any other way. There were small organisations of amateur naturalists who could well be keen to join us in exploring these difficult to reach places. (In 1963 the RSPB had a membership of about 40,000. At the time of writing it has increased exponentially to more than 1,000,000.)

Some four weeks later, we met in Torridon, one of our favourite places. As we walked around Liathach, we spoke of how we could get the whole thing off the ground. No one had attempted this kind of thing in Scotland before so we were in unknown territory. We decided that we ought to concentrate our attentions on Ross-shire and Sutherland for these were the counties at that time which were the most difficult for the individual to reach and explore on their own. A set-up like ours could be very attractive. It would be very easy for me to move my young family up north for at that time we lived in a caravan. (Yes, even then finding a house in early married life was difficult.) For us it was the only way possible to live out of town. Towed by my old Land Rover, we could transfer our home into the heart of the North West in just a matter of hours.

For Derek it would be rather more involved. He would have to sell up everything in the south and find a house within striking distance of the high hills. The actual shape of the courses we were to run was still rather nebulous. We were discussing such an idea before conservation became a popular word. The kind of people we were hoping to attract belonged to a fairly small band of keen naturalists scattered thinly throughout Britain. It was obvious that it was going to be a hard struggle. We were under no illusions that we ourselves had a great deal to learn before we set up such a project and decided that the sooner we started, the better. Later that same year, we were settling into our new life north of Inverness. If we were to make full use of the vast area at our disposal, it would be vital for us each to have a minibus apiece so that our respective groups could be transported quickly to the remotest parts of the east and west coasts along with access to the high tops so that a full day could be had on foot, exploring the natural world.

The purchase of the buses took away what little capital we had but this was the least of our problems, for we were immediately catapulted into a Kafkaesque situation when we applied to the Traffic Commissioners for permission to run both minibuses in the Highlands with a passenger service licence. In our naivety, we had no idea how very, very tightly this was regulated back then. We received a courteous invitation to attend a meeting to discuss our application which we wrongly assumed would be a formality where we would sit around a table and chat about our aims and purpose. We were horrified to discover on our arrival that it was a formal court hearing and that all the big guns of the Highland Omnibus Company and the Scottish Bus Group were brought to bear on us in the form of an Edinburgh QC. We were totally unprepared for such an event and stuttered and stumbled our way through an explanation of what we hoped to do.

The problem was that since no one had attempted such a strange idea before, our purpose was thoroughly misunderstood. We were accused of taking the bread from the collective mouths of the bus groups though we protested that it was NOT our intention to run bus tours. Our aim was to run natural history courses of which a mini-coach was only an incidental part. The outcome was a foregone conclusion. After being examined by the QC on the routes we would take across the Highlands, it was discovered in our application that we had missed a vital road from Inverness northward and since it was impossible to reach the other routes without traversing this section, the application was dismissed out of hand.

Fifty-odd years on, we still look back on this episode with a certain amount of horror. Here we were attempting an escape to a simple life but still being ensnared by bureaucratic machinery. At the end of the hearing, as the others were leaving, the QC beckoned us across to have a word. It turned out he was very sympathetic to what we were trying to achieve and apologised for thoroughly destroying our case. He suggested we make another application as soon as possible, making absolutely sure we have every route in the Highland area covered. He believed the bus companies would not spend another QC fee for such a small return. He was absolutely right. Our second application was thoroughly researched and we put up a strong case that we had no interest in competing with large bus companies. Our interest lay in the outdoors and our application sailed through much to our great relief.

In the meantime, we set about the task of getting to know our chosen territory much more intimately and spent happy days wandering across hill and glen. To eke out our by now slender resources, we hired out our buses for transporting small groups to dances, functions and weddings and in the depths of winter carried skiers from the newly opened winter sports development at Aviemore to the slopes of Cairngorm.

In those early days, we would often sit down on a sunny hillside and think of the drudgery we would be experiencing at that moment, had we not made the vital decision. We were often asked whether it took courage to throw up everything for such a crazy scheme. The answer of course is that courage played no part whatsoever for the only alternative was a lifetime of unfulfilled dreams, doing work we loathed. If we failed, we at least had the grim satisfaction of knowing that we had tried.

With diligent advertising, we managed to attract a number of adventurous souls to the Highlands for our first season but it was quite evident that it would take us a few years to build up a reputation which would enable us to make this a full time occupation. We would have to struggle on, taking work where we could find it, while all the time gaining more experience on all aspects of the Highland scene. Though it was a difficult time financially, we had the satisfaction of knowing we held the future in our own hands and were free of the shackles of industry. We had had a reasonable first season but had not earned enough to see both families through the winter. We would have to hire out the buses as a taxiing service. The idea of the minibus was catching on. It was the ideal method of transporting small groups to various functions, something we take for granted today.

One wedding we were hired for I remember particularly well, for I enjoyed it as much as the guests I carried. The phone call asked that I pick up the first person a few miles out of Inverness and he would guide me round the various addresses in the town, picking up the various passengers in turn. As I drew up to pick up my first passenger, I noted he carried a fiddle case under an arm and assumed he would be playing at the wedding. He was still casually dressed and as we drove off, he explained that they were all travelling in casual clothes and dressing at the bride's house at Poolewe on the west coast for the wedding was going to take place there. He sat alongside me in the front passenger seat and laid his fiddle carefully on the cowling of the engine which was between us. It is important to understand a little of the layout of the Thames minibus at this stage. The bus could take 11 passengers and to make it as compact as possible, the designers had placed the engine in line with the front wheels which meant that there was no bonnet. The driver, engine and front passenger all sat in one line. This meant that the single front passenger was kind of restrained in a well between the engine and the door, this early form of bus being quite narrow. The seats behind were a mixture of single and double with a sliding door for access.

Following my passenger's directions, we travelled the various streets and slowly the seats were filled until we had about eight people behind us. As we drew up at the last house, this man emerged with a beautiful accordion. They were all, of course, well acquainted with each other and it was obvious that they had knowingly left a double seat for the accordionist. What I hadn't expected was that he immediately struck up a reel and all my passengers began beating their feet in time as we drove through the town. Out of the corner of my eye, I could see that the fiddler was desperate to join in but there seemed no way he could possibly play a fiddle in that confined space. However, he was nothing if not inventive. Noting that the window was a sliding one, he opened it wide, got his fiddle out and was able to use the bow out through the window and so join in with the accordionist, albeit holding the fiddle very awkwardly. I suspect they had all been imbibing before the bus arrived for the bus was reverberating wildly with the sound of accordion, fiddle and stamping feet. Glancing in my rear-view mirror, I could see with amusement people turning to gape in amazement as we passed, as we crossed the Clachnaharry bridge leaving the town. I could swear the bus was bouncing too.

This was 1964 and every road beyond Garve was still single track so it took quite some time to travel the distance to Poolewe but my passengers had come well prepared for the journey, for the whisky was being passed freely around and I would say we were averaging about 20 miles to the bottle. We entered the village of Poolewe in triumph two hours later to the tune of The Atholl Highlanders March to Loch Katrine and drew up in happy mood at the door of the bride's mother.

Naturally, things were already hectic there. People were darting in and out of every room and another deluge of happy bodies was probably the very last thing they wanted but such is the incredible hospitality of the Highlands, everyone was welcomed with open arms and ushered into the already crowded house. Every few minutes on the journey across, one or other of my passengers would commiserate that since I was driving, I was unable to join in the festivities and this was related to the lady of the house. Though the poor woman already had enough on her plate, she plied me with tea which I accepted gratefully.

Ensconced by the fireside, I could watch with interest the antics which must happen in every household with a wedding in the offing. There was lots of scurrying round as people tried to find a private place to change into their finery. Privacy was a luxury no one could afford by this time, however, the time for the ceremony was approaching rapidly. It was only in the tiniest room in the house that a limited time was permitted alone, and even this was monitored, for there was a perpetual queue which never seemed to diminish. A discussion arose among the party as to how they should arrive at the church. I discovered that it lay less than a few hundred yards away. One group said it was daft to get into a bus only to emerge again before I could get into second gear, while the others said they must arrive in some style in the bus. I protested that I didn't mind in the least driving them the short distance if it was the proper thing to do and at last it was agreed that they would arrive in some semblance of grandeur. Just as we were leaving, some panic concerning the bride, who was hidden away somewhere, sent everyone scurrying even faster. What it was exactly, we never discovered, for our party was already cramming into the bus but it was to have a considerable delaying effect on the bride's arrival at the church.

Once everyone was seated in the bus, we drove solemnly down the road in first gear and drew up at the church door where everyone dismounted sedately again. They had all been adamant that I should attend the ceremony and after much protest, I had agreed that once they were safely deposited at the church, I would find a place to park the vehicle a short distance away and slip into the back, unnoticed. It seemed everyone in the surrounding area was attending the wedding, for there were vehicles of all types everywhere and it took me some time to find somewhere to leave the bus. As I walked back, I could hear the organ playing and hurried lest I make some noise slipping in behind if things had already begun.

It was a tiny church. I think it was one designed by Thomas Telford for the Highlands and I turned the door handle quietly, assuming it would be just like most on the east coast where you go in the door and the pulpit is at the far end and the congregation facing it. To my horror, as I stepped inside, I was confronted by about 300 pairs of eyes for this church was reversed. Even worse, the elderly woman at the small organ had assumed this was the bride arriving and struck up the Wedding March only to convert it again immediately. There seemed nowhere to sit or stand and I stood there in some confusion until someone in the bride's family waved me across and everyone shuffled along, allowing me to squeeze between them and sit throughout the ceremony in embarrassment, fearful someone would fall off the end of the pew.

Thankfully, it was a fairly short ceremony and as the bride and groom left the church, I could hear a piper striking up and the hemmed in congregation left the building, feeling some relief in being able to breathe normally again. Outside, the bride, groom and piper were waiting for everyone to form into a long crocodile, for they were going to progress round the shore of Loch Ewe to the restaurant – at that time inside the gates of Inverewe Gardens on the other side of the bay. I went back for the bus and followed the procession and was amused by how someone would break away from the main procession, do a jig and rejoin it again. The air was filled by the sound of the pipes and the banter of the guests.

The meal and speeches over, there was little time spent on formality. Tables were cleared and carried away, chairs were pulled back to the wall and my new found friends, the fiddler and accordionist, took up their position at the head of the hall and in no time, everyone was whirling to an eightsome reel, jig and Gay Gordon. The whisky flowed, laughter grew louder and the babble of voices increased in volume as the evening progressed. By one in the morning, only about half the original party could stand the pace and eventually everything ground to a halt. My passengers climbed wearily into the bus and it was as though they were all somehow connected to my ignition, for as soon as I started the engine, all heads dropped on their chest and there wasn't a sound until I reached Inverness, each emerging from the bus to walk unsteadily to their door.

But though we had to do some weird work to make ends meet, we never forgot that the main event was to build up our guiding work.

CHAPTER SIX

From Ross-shire with Love

THE CONCEPT OF taking groups of naturalists to various locations in different parts of the Highlands was a very new one back in the early 1960s. The basic idea of travelling by minibus to a location, then spending the whole day on foot looking at wildlife proved however to be an attractive one and we spread the word by advertising in magazines and by personal contacts. We did a lot of planning and research before our first season in 1964.

We had chosen Mid Ross as a base, for it had several advantages. First it was within easy reach of Inverness for picking up and setting down clients at the railway station at the beginning and end of each week. But most of all, we could take advantage of being within easy reach of both east and west sides of the country, so were able to listen carefully to weather forecasts for the following day and could do one of several things. If we saw rain was coming into the west later in the day, we would head east into the Cairngorms or on to one of the Firths. If it was already raining in the East, we were fairly sure it would clear from the west and if we drove to Wester Ross, within an hour or so we could get the better weather earlier. This we found worked very well and it became quite a joke that we would never say where we were going the next day for, to be honest, we didn't know ourselves until we heard the late evening forecast.

We always did our homework for the coming season by looking around the whole area and establishing where the wildlife was likely to be the most interesting for the coming year. Quite a large number of the birds were very reliable and came back to the same sites year after year, but populations did go up and down so we liked to be up to date.

We had started off the business by calling it Kyle and Glen which of course referred to the Kyles and Glens we would be visiting.

However, many people thought these were our surnames. After the second or third year we decided to change the name to Highland Safaris and we kept that name till our retirement. Our routine changed too. For the first two or three years we worked together on the same week but such was the difficulty of hotels at the time fitting in 24 people, we decided we split up, and while one of us took a group to Sutherland, the other took another group in Ross-shire. The following week we would change over, comparing notes on the Saturday at the end of each week so that we each knew where anything had changed, a new bird or a rare plant etc.

Wester Ross was always the favourite part of Ross-shire for it had the combination of sea and hill which produced the greatest variety of landscape and wildlife. Most people were very keen to get onto a hill, where they felt they had really achieved something. We had to grade this carefully, as most of our clients, though outdoor people, were not climbers. The hill which met all the criteria was Stac Pollaidh in Wester Ross. It is just about 2,000ft high with a jagged top and gave the impression of being a difficult climb but it was not particularly difficult. One could start the climb straight off the Achiltibuie road and though steep, if one took it slowly, most people could get on top without too much difficulty.

Being slightly lower than the Sutherland hills just over the county line, the Stac had lost its quartzite top, a very hard rock which tops all the other Sutherland hills. The quartzite protects the Torridonian Sandstone, a very ancient rock underneath. Without this protection, Stac Pollaidh had weathered into a very jagged outline. The view from the top makes the climb very much worthwhile for to the north lie all the distinctive Sutherland hills. Across the heavily glaciated Loch Sionascaig lies the long ridge of Suilven which is mostly photographed from Lochinver where it shows as a sugar loaf and seems almost unclimbable, but the view from Stac Pollaidh reveals there are several easy routes to the top. Behind Suilven one can see the many summits of Quinag while round to the right are the tops of Canisp, Cul Mor and Cul Beag. It's a strange landscape deeply cut by ice. The theory is that the quartzite was so tough, it resisted the wearing effect of ice which could only excavate the sides of the Torridonian sandstone mountains. It is thought that the glaciers of the west excavated deeper because, even in the depths of the ice-age, the Gulf Stream still had the effect of raising the temperature a degree or two, which meant the bases of each glacier were lubricated by water and they moved faster and wore quicker.

On another day of the week, we would almost certainly travel as far as Achiltibuie, where we would arrange to meet Ian MacLeod. Ian had a superb wooden clinker built boat at this time. I would guess it would have been 40 or 50ft long and he used it for fishing for prawns. He would go out early in the morning lift and re-bait his creels, then return to Old Dornie to hose down the whole boat and make it ready for taking a trip out to the Summer Isles.

We would sail out past Isle Ristol and head down to Tanera Mor where Frank Fraser Darling spent some of the war years. Fraser Darling was one of the founders of the conservation movement spending some time in Dundonnell studying deer, then on Priest Island another of the Summer Isles before settling down on Tanera Mor. He had taken over a house and the old fishing station in the bay called The Anchorage, taking some time to repair the pier which had been in full use during the time of the herring, now long gone. That had only been some 20 years before but already it was going back to nature. It was to be much later that the island would be bought and the houses restored.

There were occasions when we would visit Carn nan Sgeir, a tiny twin island joined by a storm beach. There used to be several black guillemots and an excellent tern colony here but many years later, so many people were landing there that the terns moved out and found a quieter place to nest. Sailing back north-west, we would squeeze between Tanera Beg and Eilean Fada Mor. In the early part of the year we were often fortunate enough to find a basking shark in here for they seemed to like the shallow water between the islands to rest. On occasion Ian would manage to get right alongside and it was only then one fully comprehended its bulk, which became awesome when it actually moved off.

In those early days, the only way into Applecross was over the 2,000ft pass Bealach na Ba. There was no way in from the north for the road then terminated on the south side of Loch Torridon. Consequently, the high pass was often blocked by snow in the winter. As soon as the road was open we would drive up to the summit, sometimes squeezing between high drifts by the roadside. From its summit there are extensive views to the west over the peaks of Skye and Rum, and if the weather was clear, to the Outer Isles beyond.

From the road summit, it is possible to climb even further to the top of Sgurr a' Chaorachain. In the very early spring, this can be quite good fun for this was the easiest place to take our groups to find ptarmigan in winter and spring plumage. We would spread everyone out in a long line and advance up the hill, walking very slowly and stopping occasionally to scan around with binoculars, for it is very easy to miss the birds against the snow. Then someone would give a yell as a bird would fly up at their feet. We were never sure who had the biggest fright here but I think it would have been the person. It was our job then to carefully watch the flight of the bird and note exactly where it came down. It now became something of a military exercise to spread everyone in a wide circle around the landing area and slowly walk inwards, decreasing the circle as we went. Once the actual bird was picked out we would take a small step at a time until we were just close enough to give everyone a close view through binoculars without disturbing the bird which was quite sure its camouflage was so good, we couldn't possibly see it.

Occasionally, everything worked against us. Arriving on the top sometimes in sleet or snow, only the hardiest of the group would venture out. Visibility made it very difficult to find any ptarmigan but on returning to the vehicle, we would be told that one of these birds had been sheltering on the leeward side of the vehicle and those inside had had the best view.

It was on one of these trips that we were sitting by the side of Loch Kishorn waiting for the cloud to clear off the Bealach na Ba.

We had been watching eider and red breasted mergansers on the water when something white attracted my attention to the pass through to Sheildaig. To my surprise, it was a gannet. It's quite unusual in itself to see a gannet fly over a large land mass for they tend to stick to the sea passage, but it appeared to be trailing something behind it. On training the binoculars on the bird we discovered it had a length of bright orange nylon rope attached to one foot. We all watched as it headed towards us and finally alighted in the water just in front. It sat there for a time while we discussed what we could possibly do to help. But of course there was no way we could approach it in fairly deep water. Eventually the bird made as if to fly off but the drag of the rope meant it couldn't gain enough speed to launch into the air. It then did a most unlikely thing. It reached around behind, picked up the end of the rope in its mouth and tried to take off again. With the short-ened rope there was much less drag and it lifted off the water and was away. Once safely aloft, it dropped the rope end and disap-peared towards the mouth of Loch Kishorn. It's a mystery how the bird had worked out the mechanics of what it had to do but I doubt with this handicap it would have lived very long, for gannets depend on their sleek aerodynamics in diving into the sea from some height to feed properly. It was just an instance of how damaging a careless casting aside of a piece of rope can have devastating effects on wildlife.

Torridon is one of the most spectacular areas of Wester Ross. Its mountains, Beinn Eighe, Liathach, and Beinn Alligin rise from sea level to 3,000ft in a great upward sweep of rock. It's a Mecca for climbers today but in the early 1960s it was a reasonably quiet place. Depending on weather, we would often walk round behind Liathach. It's a really remote spot which for some reason I always associate with Emperor moths for we often came across the larvae here, quite large, pale green with red on the end of its spines and just as often the tiger beetle, again green with pink spots.

On one or two occasions, we were fortunate enough to have a very fit group who were very keen to get on to a high top so we chose Beinn Alligin which can make very enjoyable circuit. Starting off from the highest car park, it's a case of toiling up through the corrie to Tom na Gruagaich and then following the ridge round to Sgurr Mhor where there is a great gash right down the mountainside. A landmark like this has to have a legend attached of course and the story is that the greatest hunter of the giants who used to live around here was chasing an equally giant wild boar. The giant caught up with the boar on top of Sgurr Mhor and as they wrestled, the boar threw its head back and slashed the giant's throat with its tusk. The giant had just enough strength before he died to throw the boar over the edge of the cliff and that great scar is where the boar's tusk tore out a gash as it fell down the mountainside. Further round the circuit we come on to the Horns of Alligin. This part is a bit of a scramble but easy enough for any fit person then it's an easy descent and walk back to the carpark. It makes a very enjoyable day.

Wester Ross is a wonderful place for black throated divers. Their approach to nesting is somewhat different to the red throated diver. While the red throat will more often nest on a small lochan and take its food back to the nest from either a very large loch or the sea, the black throat usually chooses a very large loch where it can both fish and nest. Both divers evidently haven't changed their shape for two million years. They are so efficiently designed for living in water that coming in to nest is quite a difficult time. Their legs are set so far back on the body, perfect for propulsion in water, that they cannot walk on land, so they very quietly dive and come up close to the nesting site. In the shallows they shuffle on to land, then by pulling the legs under them, they lunge forward and pull the legs up again to fall forward again till they reach the nest only a few feet from the water's edge. They sit there watchfully and at the slightest sign of danger, they push off with their feet and slide very fast and low into the water and dive immediately.

Their method of diving is so very efficient compared to that of, say, a shag. While the shag usually makes a little jump off the surface to drive itself under, the diver seems able to express all the air from the feathers and simply submerges with hardly a ripple. Sometimes this is a good way of identifying one from the other if you are against the light and a long way off.

Gruinard Bay is quite a good place early in the year to see the great northern diver. They don't normally nest on the British mainland and they spend the winter in the waters to the south around the Bay of Biscay. They start heading north again in early spring and are usually in their winter plumage at this stage. It can be difficult to distinguish it from the black throated diver in winter for it too is in the same state, so you need something to compare it with, for the head on the great northern is very much heavier. As they come into their summer plumage, they are again fairly similar with beautiful black and white diced markings on the back, but again it is the head and throat you have to look for. While the throat on the black throated has a black shield pattern, the great northern has a distinctive ring round the neck and is much the larger bird.

Gruinard Bay is only one of the many places you might see the great northern, for they appear in almost every sea loch on the western sea board, as they slowly make their way northwards to their nesting areas nearer the Arctic. It was while in Gruinard Bay late in the season one year that we coincided with the young of the black throated diver which, just having left the nest, were spending some time learning the tricks of life in the sea. They had completed the journey from the fresh water nesting site safely but were obviously having some difficulty in rising from a choppy sea to flight. Their problem was judging exactly the right time for a take-off and we saw several miscalculated mishaps. They would lift off on the crest of a small wave but couldn't get enough height before a slightly higher wave hit them sending head over tail into the sea again. It looked potentially lethal but they simply shook themselves down and made another attempt, eventually succeeding.

The eastern seaboard of Ross-shire though more domesticated has its great attractions nevertheless, for there are the bottle nosed dolphins of the Moray Firth, easily seen from the shore and good mudflats for waders. There used to be an excellent heronry near Munlochy Bay, probably the best I have ever seen, where you could stand near the edge of a cliff and look down into the tops of trees where there were regularly up to 26 nests. However, over the course of several years, the bird droppings killed off the trees and they had to move elsewhere. The woodland birds are good here too. But over our lifetime Derek and I have seen massive changes in populations. In the early days we used to do bird counts on this side of the country for the then Nature Conservancy and as an example, on a loch quite near where we lived we regularly counted something like 2–3,000 over-wintering wigeon. Now there are none. Populations of eider also appear to have fallen massively as have those of larks and I haven't heard a corn bunting for years. On a good two weeks in Ross and Sutherland in the 1960s we would expect to see something like 125 species. Not that we ever counted, but our clients liked to keep a tally of what they saw. I don't think we would get anywhere near that number now.

However, it has to be admitted that human frailty comes in to the equation too. For there is no doubt that advancing years takes a toll of faculties. Most people can no longer hear the high pitched deedle-deedle song of the goldcrest after the age of 50ish and perhaps our eyesight and general alertness is not quite what it was in our 20s.

CHAPTER SEVEN

Making Ends Meet: Winter Work

THE SECOND WINTER arrived and though we were steadily building up the numbers of clients for our summer expeditions, it would still prove necessary for us to take on some kind of winter work. This was normally quite difficult in the Highlands but luckily a temporary job came up of driving a sheep lorry for one of the local estates and I jumped at the opportunity, for it would bring in badly needed funds and a lot of the work, of course, would be outdoors. It's no good pretending I was much good at the job. In fact, it's surprising the estate manager was tolerant enough to keep me in employment throughout the whole winter. Whatever my short-comings, I must say the work was thoroughly enjoyable. Being a townie and an engineer I had never handled sheep before, so it was a steep learning curve.

On my first day, I was directed to an enormous lorry capable of carrying three decks of sheep and was told to make my way up to the head of the local glen where I would find the shepherds of the estate working at a sheep fank. It was one of those beautiful days in autumn where the sun shines from a clear blue sky, follow-ing a slight overnight frost but without the haze one usually asso-ciates with an equivalent day in summer. The surrounding hills stood out boldly in their seasonal garb of golden bracken and browning heather. The trees of the glenside were exquisite in the multiplicity of their colouring. Aspens in a delicate shade of lemon, birch which lit up even the shadowed side of the glen with their yellow brightness, rowans and geans, the richness of their red leaves only outshone by the brilliance of the heavy crop of berries and the whole interspersed with the deep solid green of the Scots Pines. It was a joy to be out on such a day.

An hour's drive took me to the head of the glen where I could see the milling mass of blackfaced sheep, contained in the sheep fank. Four shepherds were leaning over a fence, obviously awaiting my arrival. They had been out at first light, gathering the sheep off the hill in good time for the sale.

After a brief greeting, I thought it wise to admit my ignorance of sheep transport. They all laughed and assured me there was nothing to it and showed me how to operate the gates and ramps which allowed the sheep to be moved from one deck to the next, and with the help of the dogs, we had the sheep loaded in no time. One of the shepherds jumped in beside me and we were off cautiously down the glen.

It was a single track road and almost exactly the width of the lorry, so I was travelling very cautiously, for I immediately discovered that the sheep were peculiar animals in that when going round corners, they didn't lean in against the gravitational pull, the result being the lorry heeled over alarmingly on every bend. This wasn't as easy as it looked.

The shepherd laughed, 'Don't worry, you'll soon get used to it.' It was true. By the time we had reached the main road, I was better able to judge speed and angle of bend a little better. Nevertheless it was a slow journey into town and the mart was really bustling with sheep and lorries. Conscious of my lack of knowledge, I relied heavily on the accompanying shepherd to help with the unloading and soon we were on the return journey to the head of the glen for another load. By this time I was beginning to get a little more confident and with the help and good humour of the shepherds, actually starting to enjoy it. Naturally, it was expected that I would help them if the need arose and I was shown how to handle the blackface sheep by getting astride it at the shoulders and grabbing the fleece or horns. That way you could guide a recalcitrant sheep to go in the necessary direction.

This new found knowledge somewhat backfired a little later in the year. The estate had a flock of cheviots which they kept on the lower ground and I gathered they were rather special and of a very high quality. It was decided that a group of the cheviot rams were to be sold and they were expected to fetch a very high price. One morning, the estate manager told me to go to a field fairly close by, where the shepherds would be waiting, for this was the day of the big sale. The field sloped down to a hedge with the only gate at the top end where the shepherds were waiting. They were all very smartly dressed for they were taking the day off and going into Inverness to see the sale in progress. Everyone expected the price to be a new record.

We secured the ramp and ensured there was no escape for the rams. It was only then I noticed there were no dogs, for the shepherds were going to follow me directly into Inverness and they didn't want the dogs to be in the vehicles for the rest of the day. There were, I think, five of us, as we strolled down past the rams to the foot of the slope. We then spread out and I was placed out on the left wing as we slowly moved the rams up the slope to the waiting vehicle. It was all going well until we were quite close to the gaping entrance to the lorry.

Then one ram decided, 'I am definitely NOT going in there,' and made a break for it.

Of course, it had to be on my side, and the shepherds shouted, 'Get that one, Allister!'

I put all my newly acquired skills into action, grabbed the ram by the fleece near the shoulder and got firmly astride it. But my puny weight was no match for the ram and next moment I was charging down the field at what felt like 50 miles an hour on the back of this bucking animal. The ram made a stop turn at the bottom edge of the field and I was thrown off near the hedge. As I scrambled on to my feet, I looked towards the top of the field and all the shepherds were falling about laughing, and of course they had allowed all the other rams to escape too.

We all gathered at the foot of the field again and one shepherd said, 'We'll put you in the middle this time.' And we started to move the rams up the hill again but inevitably one of the shepherds would start giggling which would set off the others, the rams would escape and we had to start all over again. It took another three attempts to get the rams in the lorry, without us all collapsing with laughter, but at last it was done and the rams did indeed break all records at the sale.

My next task was even more of a problem, for I was told that since it was the end of the stalking season, I was to go up to the head of the glen and pick up two ponies which were used to carry the carcases off the hill and return them to the Ormistons in Newtonmore, who were well known in the Highlands for their expertise with the highland pony. If I knew little of sheep, I knew even less of ponies. I had to remove the decking used to carry sheep which left a roomy interior for the transport of the two ponies. My instructions were to call in at the shepherd's house and he would tell me more. The shepherd had heard the lorry arriving and was already at the door of the house, as I jumped down off the lorry.

'Where are these ponies?' I asked.

The shepherd came right out of the house, went round to the gable end, shaded his eyes and pointed high up the hill and said, 'There they are, just above the tree line.' I, too, shaded my eyes and could just make out two dots which could be ponies near the top of the hill.

'How am I supposed to get two ponies down from there?' I asked.

The shepherd turned around, went into the barn and re-appeared with two bridles. 'There you are. You just put these on and lead them down.' It sounded suspiciously easy.

Armed with the two bridles, I climbed steadily up the hill and the two dots resolved into ponies, who continued to graze quietly, as I approached. I thought perhaps this might be easier than I had expected. When I was about ten yards away, I realised they had been watching my progress with interest and suspecting that I was intent on making them do something rather than being allowed to browse quietly, they moved off at a leisurely pace. When I stopped, they stopped and when I moved forward, they would move off again. This was getting me nowhere and I decided to go back to the shepherd again.

Explaining my predicament, I said, 'Any ideas of how to catch them?'

'Don't ask me,' he said. 'I'm a shepherd, I don't know anything about ponies, but what you could try is to take up a half bale of hay. I know they would love that and if you scatter it as you come down, they may follow you. I'll come up and give you a hand.' So up the hill we went again, carrying a large bundle of hay between us. Right enough, the ponies showed a bit of interest. We laid a scattering of hay on the ground and walked away as if we were not interested in their movement and when we were a safe distance away, the ponies came and each had a mouthful of better stuff than they were used to. It seemed to be working.

Trying hard not to appear interested, the shepherd and I slowly walked down the hill, scattering the occasional bundle of hay as we went. Finally, we had to look back to see the effect on the ponies and discovered that every sheep on the hill was now behind us feeding on our generous offering, with the ponies as far away as ever.

We went down the hill again to consider a new strategy.

'The trouble is, you see, there hasn't been much stalking on the hill this year and the ponies have been allowed to wander about the glen and forage for themselves. They've got out into the habit of being difficult to handle,' said the shepherd, stroking his chin. 'Tell you what. Let's have a go, using the dog.'

The shepherd was considering the problem from a professional point of view. 'We have to get them cornered somewhere, just like sheep. A place they are into before they realise it.'

I looked around the open hill. It consisted of a beautifully smooth slope with never a dip, let alone a gully, into which we could drive them. 'Where do you suggest we do that?' I asked glumly.

'Yes, it's a ticklish problem,' he said, scratching his head. 'But I remember a few years back, I had to chase a tup over this same hill and I finally caught him in the turn of a forestry fence, round the back of the hill. The best thing we can do is push them ahead of us and see if we can trap them in the same spot.'

Well, it was better than sitting here on the heather, just looking at them. So the shepherd got hold of his dog and we once again went up the hill. The ponies once again looked up at our approach and then moved reluctantly across the hill. The shepherd controlled their general direction with the dog by ordering it out right or left when the horses showed any sign of straying.

We had been walking for perhaps half an hour, when I saw, far ahead of us, the forestry fence with a young forest beyond. I could see there was indeed a turn in the fence which made a reasonably tight corner.

'Take it very slowly now,' said the shepherd, as we edged them slowly and carefully into the angle of the fence. At last, we had narrowed the angle so much there was no possibility of escape and when the horses realised they had been outmanoeuvred, they both stood meekly, while we slipped the bridles over their heads. By the time we got back to the lorry, it was late afternoon. Leading the horses into the lorry proved less troublesome than we imagined and after a welcome cup of tea at the fireside, I took my leave of the shepherd and made my way down the glen. By the time I had driven down to Newtonmore and delivered the horses, it was quite dark and late in the evening.

Next morning, I met the estate manager: 'How did you get on with the horses yesterday?'

'Horses? Oh yes, no bother at all,' I lied.

Winter at the head of the glen could be very hard and this one proved no exception. The sheep had made their own way down from the tops as the snowline crept down. Even the glen itself was under snow for a large part of the winter, with successive frosts leaving a hard crust, making it difficult for the sheep to dig through to reach the poor grass below. Very soon, the winter feed laid in for the animals was nearing exhaustion and it became necessary to take in more feed to see them through to the spring.

The usual practice was to load a flatbed lorry with bales and carry it as far as possible until the depth of snow forced us to stop. The bales were then transferred to a following Land Rover or a tracked vehicle and shuttled up to the higher reaches of the glen.

Following one heavy snowfall, we had once more to make a trip with feed. The main road leading to the glen had been cleared of snow, but the glen was going to be very bad this time and I was instructed to drive the lorry as hard as I could at the expected drifts until I could go no further. This time, the laird himself was to accompany us. We drove off in convoy, the lorry leading with its load of feed and the Land Rover following, driven by one of the shepherds with the laird as passenger. As luck would have it, the road was particularly bad. The overnight snowfall had been accompanied by a strong wind which piled up huge drifts, obliterating the road at times and making driving pure guesswork.

With the laird in attendance, a failure to reach our destination would look bad so I drove the vehicle hard at the drifts which confronted us. In consequence, the lorry bucked and lurched through the wreaths of snow. The sheer weight gave us the impetus to plough through for the first few miles but as we travelled higher, the drifts were deeper and more compacted and at last we were brought to a halt in a massive drift.

I jumped down from the cab, quite pleased that we had made it thus far but as I rounded the back of the lorry I realised that I'd lost several bales of my load due to the wild bucking. As I stared disbelievingly at my much-diminished load, the Land Rover ploughed its way round the corner and pulled up beside me. It was stuffed full of my missing bales. Every conceivable space was crammed with feed. The shepherd had evidently enjoyed the mishap for he was grinning broadly. Of the laird I could see no sign until I noticed a flat cap peeping over the topmost bale. He had felt it below his dignity to help the shepherd pick up the fallen bales and had remained firmly in his seat while the shepherd stacked them round his passenger until only the cap was visible. The peak turned in my direction and a muffled voice dryly said, 'These are yours I believe.' He did have a sense of humour then. I couldn't repress a grin as I imagined the shepherd, having exhausted all available space, turning to the laird and saying, 'I'll just put these on your lap. It's a terrible waste of space.' My final job for the estate was an unusual one. The laird had decided to sell a small estate he also owned to the south of London and since there was no livestock on the estate, he decided that it perhaps would sell easier if he stocked it with sheep – the idea being to take a lorry load of sheep from his Highland estate, all the way south of London. This was quite an undertaking in the middle '60s for there were very few motorways and it had to be done in one go to meet the laws regarding the transport of sheep at that time. The plan was for the estate manager and myself to take shifts at the wheel and take only very short breaks for food and the usual calls of nature. It was going to take forever but we hoped to get there with the sheep still in good health, for they were all in lamb.

When the laird's wife heard that we were only taking one deck of sheep, she had a great idea. She had a favourite chaise longue that she always wished had been in their house in Mayfair and it seemed the ideal opportunity to get it there with the lorry. First thing in the morning, we drew up at the laird's house and carted the chaise longue out and into the upper deck of the lorry. Then we drove round to the field where the shepherds were waiting to load the sheep into the lower deck and we were off on the great marathon.

Taking a five-hour stint apiece, it was an incredibly slow drive that seemed to go on endlessly. We stopped only when very necessary and each of us tried to sleep when the other was driving. The consequence was that it was in the early hours of the morning as we were approaching London. The estate manager was driving at the time and he woke me up saying, 'I think we have both had enough of this. I think we should try and deliver the chaise longue first and then drive on to the estate further south. It has several advantages. We won't have to drop the sheep and then drive back through London tomorrow when it's very busy. I know exactly where the house is and at this time of night, it will be traffic free. I'll stop at the next telephone box and phone the laird's wife and tell her to expect us.' This sounded perfectly reasonable to me. We were both exhausted and anything to shorten the journey would be welcome. But there was a snag which would not be apparent until we arrived at the house. We trundled through the streets of Mayfair and drew up at the laird's town house. An outside light came on and we knew exactly which house to go to. It was only when we came round to the back of the lorry that we both realised what the fatal flaw in our idea was. How did we get down the ramp on the back of the lorry, unfold the gates, lift out the chaise longue, without letting the sheep out? We tried to let the ramp down gently but it crashed hard on the tarmac and a few lights went on all around us. We then considered the problem of unfolding the gates and keeping the sheep in. The only possible way was for me to squeeze in, opening each folding gate as little as possible. I could then climb on to the upper deck and pull the chaise longue right to the edge of the lorry then squeeze out again.

The next step had to be done decisively. We had to unfold the gates quickly, keep the sheep in with our knees while lifting the chaise longue down and on to the ramp then close one gate very quickly again. At a given signal, we both moved, unfolded the gates, stepping forward immediately, got hold of the chaise longue, feeling with our knees for any stray sheep and then pulled the chaise longue on to the bottom of the ramp. We almost got away with it. But one sheep saw its chance, leapt down the ramp and bouncing on the chaise longue, vaulted neatly onto the street.

'Grab that one, Allister!' shouted the estate manager. As I lunged sideways to grab the sheep, lights were coming on all over the street by this time while lights in the laird's house were switched firmly off. I had visions of Mayfair awakening to flocks of sheep roaming the streets.

Luckily, I had managed to get a firm hold on the escaping sheep as the estate manager unfolded the gate and we managed to thrust it back with the others before any more could escape. We carried this troublesome piece of furniture up to the house where the door was swung open and we were almost dragged inside. I think the laird's wife was deeply regretting her idea. We didn't spend any more time here and we continued on to the estate which was up for sale. We arrived just as it was getting light and awoke the farm manager who broke the news that the estate had been sold while we were on our way south and the new owner didn't want any stock on the estate. We had to rest the sheep for three days and then carry them all the way back to the Highlands but I am pleased to say they all lambed successfully. However my brief experience at being a shepherd had convinced me that my chosen path as a guide was a better one.

CHAPTER EIGHT

Breakthrough: War Games at Cape Wrath

HOWEVER, THINGS were tough and we were just scraping by; I was living in a caravan, that being all that we could afford. A real breakthrough came for us when we were able to extend our work to the far North West Highlands and gain access to Cape Wrath. It was sometime early in the summer of 1964 that we had a message from Paul Brown. It said that if we were in Sutherland, could we have a meeting at his summer cottage at Ardmore? He had an idea that might interest us. We had no idea of what he had in mind but we didn't want to miss any possible opportunity, so we made a visit to his cottage. Ardmore lies above Loch a Chadh-fi, an off-shoot of Loch Laxford which involved a rather nice walk off the road near Rhiconich. With a little searching around, we eventually found the little cottage where he and his wife Yvette spent the summers.

He was, it turned out, Professor of Ceramics at Leeds University and his wife too was an artist. They evidently loved the area so much that it was their intention to live up there permanently if only they could find a way of earning a living. Paul had come across an article about our fight to obtain the necessary permission to run mini coaches freely around the Highlands and had had an idea that if he could obtain a licence, he would run a minibus service to Cape Wrath. What a stroke of luck. We had looked longingly at the Cape Wrath peninsula for we knew well there were large colonies of birds on the cliffs, the highest on mainland Britain. But there seemed no way of getting our groups there, for to reach Cape Wrath then involved crossing the Kyle of Durness in a very small boat used by the lighthouse keepers, and then a further walk of some ten miles to the lighthouse or five miles to the cliffs. We couldn't find a way of getting our groups there, spending some time on the cliffs and getting back to the mainland without it being quite an arduous day.

Paul's idea could give us the time needed to spend an excellent day on the cliffs while the general public would love to have the opportunity of reaching Britain's most north-westerly point.

So we imparted what little we knew of the machinations of the licensing board, saying that it was very unlikely that the various bus groups would raise any objection since it was such a seemingly preposterous idea and we left him with the problem of how actually to physically get a minibus onto the peninsula. There was a road on which the lighthouse keepers used a vehicle so they must at some point have found a way of transporting it across the Kyle of Durness.

Paul had obtained the licence without any problem. He now contacted Donald Morrison, the ferryman for the Lighthouse Board. He too was very enthusiastic, for anything he earned from ferrying the general public was his to keep. Not only that, he possessed the knowledge of how to get the minibus across. So the winter of 1964/65 was spent constructing a huge raft on the shore of the Kyle. It consisted of a series of 50-gallon oil drums lashed on to a system of planks on which the minibus would be precariously balanced. All they had to do then was wait until suitable weather in spring.

All the insurance companies understandably refused to underwrite such a project and they were left with the additional worry that if anything went wrong halfway across and the bus went down, it would be a total write-off, for even at low tide, they could never extract the vehicle from the soft sand. In some way to offset this possibility, Paul placed a case of whisky in the bus, saying that if Donald got it across safely, the whisky was his. If not, the whisky went down with the bus. He needn't have worried for Donald was a very skilful boatman. And a great lover of whisky.

At last, the perfect weather arrived in the spring and at the lowest state of tide, the bus was driven down the slipway and on to the raft which sat on the soft sand. Then on a windless sunny day at the highest state of the tide, the raft was allowed to float free. Donald fixed a towline to the boat and with Hugh, his son, operating the outboard motor and Donald and a friend rowing, they edged slowly across the unruffled water. The main worry was that any breeze could topple the whole rig into the sea. But at last they reached the far shore and with the aid of planks drove the bus triumphantly onto the jetty on the other side. I am told there was great rejoicing in which the whisky played a major part.

The bus service was immediately popular, as large numbers of people were keen to visit an area hitherto not accessible and to say they had reached this remote part of our islands. Donald had the difficult task of controlling the visitors eager to cross for he could only take a small number at one crossing of the Kyle. But it was here he showed his strength for he had an authoritative way about him, no doubt a remnant of his police experience. We will hear more of Donald and his family later.

The high cliffs of the Clo Mor on the north-facing side of the peninsula offered the greatest attraction for us. Naturally our groups wanted to get to the lighthouse as well, so if it was early in the season, we would commandeer the bus and take our group to the lighthouse then immediately return about halfway back again to where a track led down to Kearvaig beach below the Clo Mor Cliffs. The short steep walk leads you down to one of the most beautiful and remote beaches in Scotland. The sands of Kearvaig face almost due north into the Pentland Firth with the hard granite gneiss of the Cape Wrath tip to the west and the overwhelming cliffs of Torridonian Sandstone to the east. The colouring here in early summer is hard to believe with the bright emerald of the sea breaking white on the shore, contrasting strongly with the dark red sandstone cliffs. The idyll is completed by the constant movement of tens of thousands of nesting seabirds. From April to July the cliffs are a seething mass. Guillemots, razorbills, puffins, shags, fulmars and kittiwakes all vie with each other in finding a suitable nesting ledge, their combined voices filling the air with sound.

The Torridonian sandstone is by far the birds' most popular nesting surface. It weathers in just the right way. When a piece breaks off the main cliff, the cleavage is always at a right angle, forming the perfect ledge for a nest site. It was interesting to note that with the help of a geological map, one could easily locate most of the main colonies in the north west. Cape Wrath is a good example of this. On the Clo Mor Cliffs to the east of the beach, there is so much overcrowding that when a bird alights, it usually knocks several others off the ledge. On the other side of the beach, on the Gneiss, apart from where the kittiwakes rest, there are only the occasional pair of fulmars and shags who manage to find a spot on the knobbly hard surface.

On the edge of the beach lies Kearvaig, one of the remotest houses on the British mainland. At this time in the later part of the 20th century, the house was empty and only used by the shepherds when they were on the Cape-side to dip the sheep or to round them up for shearing etc. It is only in the last few years when the house was being converted into a walkers' bothy that the full extent of its age became apparent. Hugh Morrison, (Donald's son) had told me the story of how one of his forebears had carried all the building materials by boat under sail and oar from Rispond, a small harbour on the west side of Loch Eriboll, all the way past Faraid Head and then across the head of the Kyle of Durness and under the Clo Mor to beach the boat on the sand of Kearvaig. He had then manhandled the building stone and materials up the beach for its construction. I had assumed it had been within living memory but it turns out that messages found within the walls when the building was being converted to a bothy revealed that it was contemporary with the lighthouse which started operation in 1828.

After lunch, if the tide was right and our group fairly agile, we would edge around the foot of the cliffs and being very careful on the still wet slippery boulders, make our way gingerly through an open ended cave which leads on to a dry flat shelf. A few steps along this and there seems to be an impregnable vertical wall of rock but with a horizontal notch through which one can wriggle flat on the stomach. This in turn leads on to a slightly higher flat shelf where we could all sit comfortably and take in the full majesty of the cliffs above. One look at the faces of those who get there shows that the scramble is worthwhile, for one is fully exposed to the cacophony of sound reverberating off the cliffs' walls and all around one's head is a swirling mass of bird life.

Sometimes, our clients enjoyed it so much it was difficult to drag them away again before the tide rose. Once, at the end of June, when seabird activity was at its height, Derek and I were keeping a careful watch on the slow creep of water towards the foot of the cliff until eventually we suggested that we ought to make the return journey. The others nodded in agreement but just then a great skua began to harry a kittiwake at very close quarters. Naturally, it caused great excitement. The skua is a pirate who earns a living by chasing other seabirds till they are forced to disgorge the fish they carry back to the chicks, whereupon the skua retrieves and eats the catch. On occasion it will kill and eat its quarry if it refuses to disgorge.

The chase went all over the cliff and was closely followed through binoculars by the excited group. The skua, ignoring all other birds as the pair twisted and turned almost in unison – the kittiwake performing incredible aerobatics in its attempt to shake off its pursuer – mirrored every move and the exhausted kittiwake finally dropped its catch. We saw a flash of silver as the fish dropped towards the sea and the kittiwake made its escape. The skua immediately turned over in mid-flight, dived and caught the fish before it reached the water. It had been an exciting chase and every-one continued to sit and watch in the hope that the skua would pick out another victim but it was well satisfied with its recent meal and sat placidly on the water.

Derek and I continued to watch the steady rise of water. A stone we used as a guide was already well covered. Once again we suggested it was time to move and the group, with many a reluc-tant backward glance, slowly moved back along the base of the cliff. As we feared, the route through the cave and the stone beyond was already under water. It meant that everyone but the most coy had to remove trousers in order to reach the beach. By the laughter echoing round the cliff, it was clear that everyone had enjoyed the experience.

The interior of the peninsula is a mixture of boggy moor and hill. There are only two hills of any reasonable height – Sgribhis Bheinn (Scrishven) at 1,200ft and Fashbeinn (Fashven) 1,498ft.

Scrishven rises from the sea cliffs to its summit in the course of about one mile and it was our habit to climb the grassy slope from the Kearvaig beach on to the cliff top, stopping occasionally to enjoy the view to the lighthouse and out to the sometimes seen Sula Sgeir on the horizon. From the highest point we would turn inland and walk on to the summit. I always felt very much at home here for the landscape and vegetation was exactly like that of the summit plateau of the Cairngorms where I had spent most of my mountaineering youth. It is composed of large areas of shattered rock and gravel interspersed with islands of dwarf juniper, clubmoss, mountain azalea, moss campion and various lichens. In fact, a sub-arctic environment. We occasionally came across Ptarmigan here at a height of 800ft, just above the sea cliff. In Ross-shire we would seldom find them below 2,000ft and in the Cairngorms below 3,000ft. On one memorable occasion, a girl in our group came across a pair of Dotterel nesting at 1,000ft – a record low at the time.

One cannot wander far across the moorland on the Cape-side without hearing the plaintive piping call of the Golden Plover. They are everywhere. Beautifully marked birds, we come across both the southern form and the northern. Of these, I think the northern form has the edge for beauty. Its back is a speckled yellow and black and its under parts are a dense black which runs up from its belly to its throat and cheek with an outline of white dividing the differing colours, giving the bird a very bold appearance. Despite this, they are sometimes difficult to spot among the heather. It can be a frustrating business to hear the continuous piping close at hand but not see the bird until it stands on a prominent knoll, determined to see you off its territory.

The Cape Wrath peninsula is owned by the Ministry of Defence and there are often naval bombardments from the sea in the spring. When this occurs, all traffic on the Cape-side is suspended and the bus has to remain at the ferry until a ring of sentries allows the public full access again. We used to see a pair of Golden Eagles fairly regularly, floating above the Cape on a thermal. But one day, I think in the 1970s, Hugh Morrison, who was driving the bus at that time, had the awaited permission to drive through the Cape after a particularly heavy bombardment. As he drove along, he noticed something sitting at the roadside. To his surprise, it was one of the eagles. He felt sure it would move off as they approached but it continued to sit in a hunched position. Even when they pulled up by the bird, it showed no sign of moving and it was only when Hugh opened the door to see if the bird was injured that its instincts made it flap with some difficulty to perch a little distance off. There was no obvious sign of injury, so Hugh decided the best course of action was to leave it and look for it again on the return journey.

Some time later, on returning to the same spot he scoured the landscape but the eagle had gone. We never saw it again round its usual haunts and we assumed it may have been caught in the blast from a shell exploding somewhere inland. Two or three years later, a new nest was reported on the Cape-side and we thought the second bird might have taken in a new mate or an empty territory had been taken over by a new pair.

To get back to Donald and Hugh Morrison. Over the years I got to know them really well for in those early days Paul didn't want the trauma of taking the bus back on to the mainland for its yearly Passenger Service Vehicle Test. It was my habit at the end of each winter to make the journey up to Durness in order to spend a few days bringing the bus up to scratch for the test when the examiner would come on to the Cape-side and do a test run on the single track Cape road. This was in everyone's interest for we wanted to be sure we had access to the Cape at all times, Paul didn't want to lose time and passengers and Donald didn't want to lose customers on the ferry.

Donald's wife was a gentle soul who always welcomed visitors. No one during the winter was allowed to pass the house without being asked in for coffee. In those days, fresh milk was unavailable so it was drunk with Carnation or condensed milk, depending on the taste of the visitor. I discovered she hated water and in all the time I knew her, I didn't once hear of her being on the mainland side of the ferry. All provisions must have been taken in by Donald. I would be lying under the bus in its winter position outside Donald's house by the edge of the cliff, engrossed in a problem with the gearbox or exhaust and oblivious to the outside world, when a voice would call me out and I would emerge into the blinding colour of an end of winter day on the Kyle, to be presented with coffee and a doorstep of a sandwich. And so I learned about Donald's life. He was a big, burly man of immense strength. A local, he had left Durness in his youth and like so many others had gone down to Glasgow to join the police force. He told me little of that period in his life except for one story.

It seemed one part of his beat was through a dockland area of Glasgow and on this particular day he kept coming across a very drunk seaman. He gave him the rough edge of his tongue and told him in no uncertain terms that if he didn't get back to his ship, he would have no alternative but to run him in. It was quite evident that the man was so stupefied by drink that he could not comprehend what was being said nor could he find his way back to the ship. Donald was unwilling to pull him in and simply kept a watchful eye on him. As luck would have it, the policeman who was to relieve him came along at that moment and as he approached, the seaman slid to the ground and fell fast asleep. Though Donald was all for letting the drunk sleep it off, the second policeman was quite determined they pull him in and very reluctantly pulled the man to his feet. With an arm apiece, they dragged him in the direction of the police station.

It was in the course of the last few hundred yards that the drunk began to come to his senses, muttering in Gaelic that surely they would not be taking him in for having a wee bit too much to drink. Donald understood of course and asked him where he came from. To his surprise he discovered that the man was the son of a crofter not far along the coast from Durness. The family had been having a difficult time and the son had gone off to the merchant navy in order to boost the income. Donald asked which boat he was on and said they would see him back to it. All this conversation of course had been in Gaelic and the second policeman had not the slightest idea of what was being said. Donald and the drunk made a neat wheelabout, using the second bobby as a fulcrum and the next moment they were walking in the opposite direction with the other bobby protesting violently and still in the dark as to what was happening. Donald was not content until he had not only taken the man to his ship but put him safely to bed.

I suspect something dramatic happened during the course of Donald's career for he had a long, deep jagged scar down one side of his neck. I never had the courage to ask him what happened but whatever it was, he left the police and came back to Durness where he secured the job of ferryman for the lighthouse board. This involved living in the ferry house situated on the Cape-side for the lighthouse keepers had to have access to the light 24 hours around the clock. In the early days, he must have used oars and sail but he was eventually given an outboard motor which was kept in meticulous condition. This made it somewhat easier to ferry the materials required to keep the road in reasonable order. So the council workers would take large amounts of gravel and tar across to the Cape-side and by hand they would make repairs to the road to the lighthouse.

Our timing often coincided with the postman delivering mail to the keepers at the light but Donald never allowed the postman to get wet feet. At the time, this man weighed at least 18 stones but whatever the state of tide, Donald would beach the boat at the lowest tide, walk back to the jetty, heave the postman onto his back and, in his turned-down waders, carry him out to the waiting boat. At the other side he would repeat the procedure, then they would walk up the hill together and the postman would disappear into the house where Mrs Morrison would give him his coffee and hear the local gossip. Then the postman would climb on to his motor bike left there for the purpose of taking the mail up to the lighthouse.

As mentioned earlier, the peninsula was used by the war department as an artillery range and in the '60s Donald used to ferry the sentries across the Kyle so they could be posted to prevent the public wandering into the range. Probably the thinking of the time was that since the Ministry of Defence was causing so much inconvenience to the people of Durness, they would at least use as much of the facilities as possible so that income to the locals was generated. On one of my visits to prepare the bus for the coming season, Donald told me he had put in his request for payment for ferrying supplies and sentries but had no recompense even on a reminder. Being Donald, he did nothing further but waited for the spring and the next bombardment. What happened then, I am sure was slightly embellished but it makes a good story. I am only sorry I didn't witness it first-hand.

The NATO fleet were sitting out in the bay and a bombardment was about to commence. A company of soldiers arrived in Durness and set up an observation post on Faraid Head, a promontory north of Durness whence at that time the bombardment was usually controlled. A platoon were marched down to the Kyle where Donald was in his usual position, sitting back against a rock, bonnet pulled down over the eyes in the bright sunlight and pipe clenched between his teeth. The platoon of sentries marched down the pier. The officer issued a few orders and a few men detached from the main group and marched down to the jetty. As the first soldier swung his leg over the bow of the boat, Donald removed the pipe from his mouth and said, 'Where do you think you are going?'.

The soldier looked at his superior, who in turn looked in surprise at Donald and said, 'Why, to post the sentries of course.'

Pointing the stem of his pipe to the boat, Donald said in a voice that brooked no contradiction: 'No one sets foot on that boat till I'm paid for last year.'

The officer blustered, 'But good God man, the whole NATO fleet are waiting out there for our signal to commence firing.'

'I don't give a damn – no one moves till I'm paid.' said Donald calmly.

The platoon were now grinning widely and the officer, conscious of his ridiculous situation, gave them a glower. He turned back to Donald and said in a reasoning voice. 'Look, why don't you take us across, I can post the sentries and then come back and discuss the situation.'

'No,' said Donald simply. 'It's got to be settled now.'

The officer was by now somewhat flustered. 'Look, I am ordering you to take us to the other side.'

'Oh, we are under martial law now are we?' said Donald raising his eyebrows and smiling.

Just then the radio operator said he was getting a signal from the exercise controller. He was enquiring if all the sentries were in position. The officer hurried to the set to say there had been a slight delay but it would be cleared up very quickly and then returned to Donald, who by this time was comfortably seated with his back to the cliff again.

The unfortunate officer said, 'You are putting me in a very difficult situation you know. How am I to explain this to my superiors?'

'I'm sorry about that,' said Donald. 'But I am not budging from here till someone pays me for my work.'

The situation seemed to be deadlocked and the officer turned to the corporal. 'Is there anything we can use to cross the Kyle?'

'No sir, since we use the ferry, the Gemini craft were not taken.'

'Can we get one from the navy?'

'There is a naval craft in Loch Eriboll sir. But it would take too long to get there and back. The exercise is due to begin in 18 minutes,' he said, looking at his watch.

Just then the radio crackled into life again. 'What the hell is going on there?' said a voice from the other end. 'The countdown has had to be suspended because you are not in position. Where are you and what is going on?' fumed the voice.

'I'm sorry sir, we are at the ferry and are having some difficulty in getting across.' The officer apologised. He could not bring himself to explain the full extent of his difficulties. By now he was desperate, he was already thinking of the laughter this would cause not only in army circles but in the navies of several European countries if it ever got out. If he didn't meet the deadline, he would somehow have to explain it. How could he possibly say that he couldn't reach his post because the ferryman wouldn't take him across. The voice at the other end said. 'I am going to restart the countdown with commencement in 30 minutes from now and you had better be in position,' snapped the voice.

As a last resort the officer turned to Donald and said, 'How much does the Ministry of Defence owe you?'

Donald mentioned a comparatively small sum and the officer said, 'If I pay you in cash, will you take us across?'

'I would be delighted,' said Donald.

The officer produced his wallet but discovered he was still a few pounds short. He offered this to Donald who shook his head. 'No, I have to be paid in full.' There was nothing else for it but to make a collection round the rest of the platoon to make up the shortfall. On being presented with his cash, Donald ushered them aboard with great ceremony and took them across. And they raced off at great speed in the minibus which they had hired for the duration of the exercise. We often wondered how the officer explained this expense to the Ministry of Defence. We did notice that the following year the army started using helicopters and Gemini craft.

One always had the feeling that Donald, whatever the situation, was in full control. My chief memory of this is of one day being caught out by a sudden change in the weather on the Clo Mor cliffs. Though the overhead conditions were fine, a gale sprang up from the north and Hugh met us with the bus at the Kearvaig road end much earlier than usual, intimating we had to get back to the ferry as quickly as possible as the crossing might be difficult. As we came down the last mile to the ferry, looking down on the Kyle,

I could see white horses kicking up. It appeared the outgoing tide was meeting the northerly gale. But down at the ferry it was all quiet for its position had been well chosen. Donald had prepared the ferry in a way I had never seen before. A massive tarpaulin was folded neatly on the bow of the boat and Donald was in his oilskins. He took particular care where everyone sat and then folded the tarpaulin over their head. He asked me to get in last and sit with him on the stern. We then edged out of the shelter of the jetty.

As soon as we were clear of the cliff, we had the full benefit of the gale and the spray from the bow was thrown well over the boat as it bucked and rolled. Our passengers couldn't see what was happening, as they were under the tarpaulin and facing towards us, but they were enjoying the movement and the sound of spray drenching the boat. I glanced sideways across to Donald but his face was impassive as ever – all he did was pull his bonnet further over his eyes and turn his pipe upside down so that the spray didn't get into the pipe. I thought it important that I too retained that impassive air for the others under cover were watching our reaction. I then realised he was not taking the usual route across but was heading into the wind all the time, only edging occasionally towards the other side. Eventually we were still pointing the bow north but edging along the mainland rocky shore. I had never been this way before by boat and could see no possible place of putting ashore. Then Donald made a sudden move and slid the boat into a narrow cleft in the rocks and jumped ashore. I helped the others ashore and as they scrambled up the rocks, Donald said in my ear. 'That's one of the worst crossings I've ever made.' That shook me a little for he had never at any time looked in the least worried.

Donald had two sons. I had never met the eldest son for, like so many others in the years after the war, he had taken the opportunity to emigrate to Canada. Hugh, on the other hand, I got to know quite well over the years. He and his brother had been some of the last to be educated on the Cape Wrath peninsula. There was a tiny school at Achiemore, about a mile and a half north of the ferry house. At that time, there had been a family living in Daill, just a little beyond the school and another at Inshore. They had had, it seems, a good primary education there.

On leaving school, work in that north-west corner as in other parts of the Highlands and Islands was very scarce and there was a tradition for its youngsters to join the merchant navy. So Hugh left home and spent several years at sea. But poor health meant he had finally to give up roaming across the world and return home where he was in the ideal position to drive the Cape Wrath bus. Hugh never looked in good health and had the occasional bout of illness. One winter, while he was still living in the ferry house, he took a particularly bad turn in the middle of the night. Donald and his wife were very worried and phoned the local doctor in Durness. Asked to describe the symptoms, it was obvious to the doctor that Hugh was bleeding internally and must be treated at the hospital in Golspie on the east coast of Sutherland as a matter of urgency. Donald would have to get Hugh across the Kyle in the middle of a dark winter's night.

They discussed the situation. Visibility was non-existent. Donald would need something to orientate him towards the mainland jetty and the doctor agreed to drive down there and shine his headlights across the Kyle, but before leaving, phoned for an ambulance for the long journey to Golspie. At that time, the ambulance was based in Kinlochbervie some 20 miles away.

Donald wrapped Hugh in several blankets and carried him in total darkness down the steep hill to the waiting boat and made him as comfortable as possible under the bow. Across the Kyle he could see the lights of the car. If the tide were high, he could simply take a straight line across – but the tide was falling and he knew the sandbanks would be breaking the surface. It must have been a gut wrenching journey for he had to rely entirely on his lifetime memory of the sandbanks and their changing patterns. From the boat, he could see the lights of the speeding ambulance as it made its way up the side of the Kyle and with this added reference point finally made it to the mainland side where poor Hugh was carted off to hospital. He survived this traumatic experience and when we arrived in the spring, he was his usual cheery self, though still a little wan.

It was sometime during that season that I had another example of Donald's authoritative manner. It was our habit to listen intently to the radio weather forecast at 6.00pm every evening and if it were a particularly good forecast I would phone Donald and suggest we take our group across the following day. On this occasion we had a very large group and it would take several trips by boat to get everyone across. When this was the case, we would arrange an early breakfast and get everyone down to the ferry a full hour before the general public arrived. This way we avoided creating a backlog of passengers for Donald at the usual starting time.

It was a beautiful morning and the ferrying was going well. We were all sitting on the grassy knoll by the side of the slipway enjoying the sun and Donald would summon down the next group of six for the next crossing. The Cape Wrath Hotel was at that time a well-known fishermen's hotel. It lay just above us as we lazed in the sun. We noticed a figure walk down from the hotel towards us and one of our group, who was in the legal profession in London, exclaimed, 'I know him. He's one of the leading QCs in London.'

To our surprise, he headed straight towards us. 'Why is everyone sitting here?' he asked.

I said we were waiting for Donald to ferry everyone across. He was instantly of the opinion that he had priority since he was going to fish on one of the lochs on the Cape-side and that as the Cape Wrath Hotel owned the fishing, Donald would take him across first.

Donald was on his way back to pick up the next load and the fisherman walked down the slipway to meet him as he came in. This was going to be interesting, but very annoyingly we were up on the knoll and just out of earshot and had to rely on body language. In his usual languid way Donald slid the boat expertly alongside the slipway and stepped ashore, pipe clenched between his teeth and bonnet pulled well down over his eyes in the morning sun. The fisherman stepped towards him and started an animated spiel. Donald stood there silently listening. When the man had stopped talking, Donald pulled the pipe from his mouth and, stabbing the stem towards the man's chest, said just a few curt words and the fisherman turned on his heel and walked meekly back up the slipway as Donald called down the next group. The QC had met his match – and knew it.

Donald retired to the family croft on the outskirts of Durness and I would see him occasionally at the peat bank and give him a wave. But he had one last adventure still to come. He and a friend would go out fishing with his own boat to a tiny island which lies off Durness. On this particular day, a heavy mist came down and Donald and his friend didn't return at their usual time, and eventually the search and rescue teams were called out. They scoured the area as best they could in the thick mist but by dark had to call off the search until the next day.

In the morning at first light, they were located almost immediately on the east shore of Loch Eriboll. They had lost their bearings in the mist and had unknowingly drifted across the head of Eriboll. On hearing waves breaking just ahead of them, they approached the shore cautiously and managed to find a landing place on a pebble beach. They had searched along the tide line and found enough drift wood to make a fire where they cooked and ate their recently caught fish and kept warm until the next morning when the searchers found them. They were not in the least worried and I think, secretly annoyed, that so much fuss had been made. If not found immediately that morning, they would have got their bearings and returned home under their own steam.

Durness sits on an outcrop of limestone which, not surprisingly, is named Durness Limestone. It has a much more gentle green landscape compared to the rugged area surrounding it and is where the main population of the area live and work. After dinner on the long summer evenings, I would stroll down to Loch Croispol or Loch Borralie. Botany had always been my weakest subject and the area round about was very good for flowers and I would try to remind myself of what I had learned from the previous year, but my brain wouldn't seem to retain much over the winter so this was at least an opportunity to look for some of the rarer flowers that most botanists would like to see on their trip to Sutherland. The limestone contained the primula scotica (Scottish Primrose) and various types of rare orchid. It was here I would occasionally meet a retired shepherd named Murdo MacKenzie. It emerged from our conversations that he was born and brought up in the house at Kearvaig.

Murdo had been a shepherd all his life. He had several brothers and they had all been born at Kearvaig where they had lived for many years. I remember him saying that it was not unusual for him and his brothers, after a day on the hill in the summer, to walk the five miles down to the ferry and cross to attend the local dance in Durness. They would return in the early hours of the morning, crossing the Kyle in semi darkness (a feat in itself) and walk the five miles home only to get up in the morning for another day on the hill.

A conversation with Murdo was always entertaining. As with quite a number of older people in the Highlands, one was never quite sure if you were having your leg pulled or not. A statement would be made in a very serious manner and your face would be studied to see if you were taken in, while you in turn studied his eyes for the slightest hint of a twinkle. If he saw you were hooked, he would string you along until he could contain it no longer and the eyes would give him away. One such tale I must confess, I am still uncertain about but since I could detect no twinkle, it may well be true. When they gathered all the sheep off the Cape-side for the sales at Lairg some 60 miles off, they would fit each sheep with a set of leather boots for the long journey.

'Leather boots!' I exploded. 'Now come on Murdo, you're pulling my leg this time!'

'Och well, if you don't believe me there is no point in telling you why,' he said seriously.

I looked hard at him but there was not a flicker of an eyelid to give me a clue. 'All right then. Why did you have to do that?'

'Well, you know what the country is like here. It's very boggy on the Cape-side where the sheep find the best grass so their feet get very soft being in water most of the time. When we used to gather them, we had to fit these leather boots because driving them south over the hills of very hard rock between here and Lairg, they wore their feet down very badly and arrived in poor condition and we couldn't get a good price.'

'You mean that every sheep you took off the Cape-side, you had to up-end and fit four boots?'

He nodded. 'Every one. The young lads today have no idea of the work we had to put in. Nowadays, they just drive them off the hill into a lorry and then sit back till they arrive at Lairg. We had to take several days to walk them down making sure they were driven slowly so they arrived in prime condition.'

'I still find that hard to believe.'

'Well, that's up to you but what I am telling you is no more than what happened,' he finished.

I scrutinised his face once more but found no clue to guide me, and I was forced to admit it was possible. The 60 miles to Lairg is the wildest and certainly the rockiest area I know in the British Isles. It would certainly be hard on the feet. On balance, I had to believe the story. On the other hand...

During another conversation, he told me that when he was a young boy, he had come across a tiny lochan hardly bigger than a puddle on which was nesting a pair of red throated divers. This pair had returned year after year until he had left the Cape some years ago. Since I would be going across in the next few days, I asked him for a description of its position. He told me how to line up Fashven with a point on the clifftop and I said I would try and find it if I could. Two days later, I found myself very close to the spot Murdo had described and out of curiosity, went to have a look. Stopping some way off, I scanned the tiny stretch of water through the binoculars and was delighted to see a red throated diver sitting on the same nest some 60 years on. When I told Murdo on my return, he was as pleased as I, and we both marvelled at the unchanging habits of wildlife. From the generations of divers' point of view, there was probably nothing marvellous about it at all. It was a perfect site where it could have a 360-degree view of the surrounding moor, there was just the right area of water to allow for a take-off and landing and there was a sea teeming with fish less than a mile off.

Sadly, when I returned to Durness one spring, I learned that Murdo had died. Over the following years while on the Clo Mor, I would often hear the quacking flight call of the red throated diver and through the binoculars find and recognise its hump back, rapid flight, head and tail down and follow it as it started its glide down to the tiny lochan with a fish in its mouth. Or occasionally I would hear its mournful, spine tingling call and think of Murdo. I wish I had retained more of what he had told me.

CHAPTER NINE

Ski Explorations on Ben Wyvis

I HAD BEEN A very keen ski mountaineer from the age of 14, for from Aberdeen the Eastern Cairngorms were within reach and with a glut of ex-army ski equipment being sold off at the end of the Second World War very cheaply, this was a relatively inexpensive way to enjoy the weekends in winter. This passion had had to take a back seat for a while as we tried to establish ourselves as guides in the Highlands. Another winter came, that of 1965/66, and there were not quite enough financial reserves for the family to survive until spring. Another quest for work was called for and luckily for us, this turned out to be a very enjoyable one for both of us, and I was able to re-engage with my youthful passion of ski-exploration.

Ben Wyvis dominates the whole of Easter Ross. It cannot be truthfully said to be an imposing mountain, for though it has enormous bulk, its long flat summit ridge detracts from any impression of height that a conical peak implies. Nevertheless, it is 3,433ft high and retains large tracts of the winter snow well into spring. It was at the beginning of that winter that Chris Harley, the then development officer for Ross and Cromarty, wrote an article drawing attention to the fact that Aviemore had been successfully launched as a winter sports centre, with most of its skiing based on Cairngorm, ten miles away. Was it not possible, he suggested, that Strathpeffer lying as it does, virtually at the foot of Ben Wyvis, might be in the ideal situation for development as a second winter sports centre, making use of the snow which lay fairly close at hand?

Developed originally as a Spa, Strathpeffer's fortunes had been a rollercoaster. Very popular before the First World War, it had been visited by many members of European Royalty but by the end of the war, its fortunes had ebbed – though had taken an upward turn for a short period following the Second World War.

This didn't last, for a new configuration of a faster road to the west meant the village was bypassed. In the 1960s a way forward for the village was badly needed. Skiing could be a possible way. The trouble was no one knew much about the winter conditions on Ben Wyvis so the hill needed to be fully surveyed. At that time, not many people skied away from the main centre at Aviemore. Ben Wyvis involved a five mile walk and an ascent almost from sea level so it was relatively unknown from the skiing point of view.

I contacted Chris and after a long discussion, it was agreed that I should climb and ski on the Ben at least one day of each week throughout the winter – which I would certainly enjoy – but best of all, I would be paid to do it. Safety was the next consideration, for this was long before mobile phones could get you out of a jam on a mountain top. It was considered necessary that I should have a companion and of course I suggested my brother-in-law Derek. At that time, Derek's winter mountain skills were minimal and it took a little time to train him up on the use of an ice axe etc, for a course on skiing would take too long. Much to his relief, his job was to accompany me on foot and take various measurements while I skied. This would have the added bonus of expanding our knowledge of winter wildlife on the high tops. So began many years of highly enjoyable winters on the Ben, which would culminate, we hoped, in a first class report on winter conditions on the mountain.

The moment the first snow fell, we set off, full of enthusiasm. There was no doubt the best approach to the mountain was from the west, starting at Garbat on the Ullapool road. From here, a gigantic unbroken steep slope sweeps up to the summit ridge. This slope took the full impact of the westerly gales which in winter are fairly prolific. As a consequence, any snow which has the temerity to fall here is picked up by the ferocious wind and deposited on the other side of the mountain. This great slope ends abruptly towards its southern end in a steep rocky drop into a glacial valley known as the Bealach (The Pass). Our route lay up the ridge of An Cabar (The Antler) where the steep slope turned on to the rocky precipice.

Hind shooting takes place over a large part of the winter and it is the normal custom when going on to any hill to be careful that the keeper's work will not be affected. Accordingly, we knocked on the keeper's door at Garbat and it was opened by a lean, slight man in his late 70s with the kind of face one usually associates with those who have spent their lives out of doors: Heavy lines around twinkling eyes caused by a lifetime of squinting against sun and snow; skin windburned to a deep, reddish brown, pulled taut against the cheekbones. Johnny Grant had spent most of his life here and knew the ground better than anyone. We explained our mission and made it clear we would always check with him before going on the hill. Johnny seemed quite interested in what we were up to and finally asked, 'Which route would you be thinking of taking?'

I said we would probably go up and back by the An Cabar ridge. Johnny mulled this over for some time and then said, 'I tell you what you should do. Go up by the ridge, you'll find the best snow is on the far side in Corrie Feithriach but on the way back, it would be best for me, if you would go down through the corrie behind the ridge, then through the Bealach and back down here.' This meant we would be making a fairly wide circle but since the corries on the other side were likely to be full of snow then it would certainly be no hardship. Our meeting with Johnny established a pattern which we followed during the hind shooting season over the years, going up by the ridge and returning by the Bealach. It was not until we were in our second or third year of our survey that it occurred to us to question the reason for the pattern. I remember we were sitting just below the summit of the Ben surrounded by acres of unblemished snow, bathed in sunshine, steadily munching sandwiches, when the conversation turned to Johnny. Derek said,

'Why do you think Johnny likes us to return by the Bealach during the hind season?'

He was thinking that he was going to be robbed of a glorious glissade down the narrow gully on the west slope. This is a method where on a steep slope and in suitable snow conditions one can sit down on a steep slope and using the ice axe as a rudder whizz down some 2,000ft of mountain in about ten minutes.

'Yes' I agreed. 'It is a bit odd, but he is usually shooting on the day we are up here because we hear the shots just as we come into the head of the Bealach.'

'It's funny we always hear the shots when we are at about the same position though.' I had noticed but put it down to coincidence. We both pondered the mystery for a moment then the light dawned on us at the same time.

'The cunning devil!' and we both laughed.

Johnny, like all the best keepers who are getting on a bit, had been using his head instead of his legs. He knew the hinds love to be at the foot of the corrie just where it turns in to the head of the Bealach. It is sheltered here and even in deep snow they can dig through to the vegetation. If the snow makes it difficult, they will come lower where the snow doesn't lie too long. By encouraging us to take this route, Johnny ensured that we would come over the summit ridge, do our exploring high up then descend towards the Bealach, pushing the hinds ahead of us. Having a fair idea of the time it would take us to make our circle, Johnny would pick up his rifle later in the afternoon, stroll up to the point where the Bealach exits to the west, find a comfortable vantage point, scrutinize each hind as they emerged and shoot those he didn't think would make it through the winter.

It was the perfect scheme, but we didn't mind in the least for we were well aware that the keeper has an unenviable job in winter, weeding out the sickly and useless hinds. Slithering around on one's stomach and lying absolutely still in deep snow and freezing temperatures in order to get a clear shot is a task few would enjoy.

It was immediately clear that the best corrie for skiing was Corrie Feithriach, directly behind the An Cabar ridge. The angles were just about right for the moderate skier though we concluded that the natural runs would have to be lengthened by the judicious use of fencing to make the snow drift into the right places. The greatest natural feature in its favour was that it faced south-east and had remarkable shelter from the ferocious winds which are the bugbear of Scottish skiing. The severe winds which raced up the western flank caused so much turbulence above the mountain that the east-facing corries experienced little or no wind at all, while the snow which was swept off the western face percolated through the turbulence and was deposited in a nice level fall over the eastern corries. This was our theory but it had to be proven and set down on paper. The only way of doing this was to take an anemometer onto the mountain in the worst possible conditions to obtain accurate measurements of wind speeds on the exposed and sheltered sides.

We waited patiently until a weather forecast showed an intense low pressure system racing across the Atlantic towards Scotland. According to the weather station at Kinloss, our nearest meteorological Station, it should hit our area about mid-morning of the next day. We spent that evening ensuring that every piece of equipment we could possibly need was properly packed.

Next morning, we arrived at Garbat as day was breaking. Though it was overcast, there was not so much as a breath of wind as we strode onto the snow covered hill. A few hard things were said about weather forecasters in general, as we panted our way up An Cabar. Climbing steadily, in an hour, we were at 2,000ft. It was our normal practice to stop at a large boulder which we christened the shelter stone, to recover our breath. There was a light breeze here and I dug out the anemometer from the rucksack and held it aloft. Ten miles per hour. There were a few more muttered words about weather forecasters as we sat with our backs to the boulder and drank a little coffee.

Just as we finished and prepared to continue the climb, it began to snow, very lightly at first, then a little thicker as the flakes grew larger. Several gusts of wind blew the snow horizontally from behind and slightly to our left. By the time we were 200ft above the shelter stone, the wind had risen to a shriek and the driving snow enveloped us completely. Conversation was impossible. We stopped briefly to don overtrousers and it was here that Derek made a slight error of judgement which would come back at us later. Instead of tucking his overtrousers under his anorak, in his hurry, he just pulled them over the top. Still another 800ft to the summit ridge and the wind was buffeting us furiously. We were in a complete and utter whiteout, where not even the next step was visible. It was potentially dangerous, for if we were unknowingly pushed to our right, we might end up on the rocky vertical outcrops of the face above the Bealach. We now understood that our theory was being put into practice. The steep west face meant the wind was actually accelerating up the slope carrying with it concentrations of snow which were not being permitted to alight on that side of the mountain. The thought of stopping, taking off a rucksack and taking out an anemometer for a reading didn't bear thinking about. We were, I think, about 200ft from the An Cabar summit when we realised we could no longer remain upright and we got down on all fours. This was even worse, for the concentration of blown snow was such that we couldn't breathe. Up on our feet again, we grabbed the shoulder straps of each other's rucksack and by moving one at a time we zig-zagged our way up to the top.

The cairn on An Cabar is tiny, no more than two feet high, since it is not the true summit but only marks the end of the summit ridge. It was the natural instinct to sit down with our back to this cairn to regain our breath and composure. But this too was impossible for we were low to the ground again and the density of blowing snow was again so much we couldn't breathe. It was only by turning inward to the cairn and sitting on our knees with our face close to the rock that we found some relief.

'You'll have no grumbles about the met office now!' Derek bawled.

Nodding, I shouted, 'No, I take it all back!' and then remembering why we were up there in those conditions, said, 'I suppose I had better take a reading.' He grinned and nodded. He knew, of course, the recorder was in my rucksack.

I rummaged in my rucksack and extracted the anemometer, sticking it out from the cairn as far as I dared. Right off the scale as we already knew it would be, for the scale only went up to 70mph. There was no doubt it was in excess of 100mph. There was no point in hanging around here. I shouted to Derek that we should go down into the potential skiing corrie to get some shelter and we stood up to go. It was then that Derek's folly became apparent, for we had to lean so far into the wind that it got into the elasticated top of his overtrousers which billowed out and next moment were around his ankles. We were both doubled up with laughter, but couldn't laugh because we were choking on snow, and we had to dive back to the cairn with our faces close to the rock before we could explode.

We both knew the ridge intimately by this time but it was certainly the worst conditions I have ever experienced on the Scottish hills. The buffeting of just lifting the foot for the next step sent you staggering in every direction and once more we had to grab each other's shoulder straps to make any headway. In this manner we struggled along the summit ridge and when we thought it safe to do so, started dropping into the south-east facing corrie.

Just 50ft below the summit, the wind dropped phenomenally. Here we felt comfortable enough to take a wind reading. It was down to 45mph and by the time we were in the middle of the corrie, it was down to 15mph. It was difficult to believe that only a few hundred feet above us, the blizzard was still fiercely raging. So our theory had been proved correct. We ran into whiteout conditions many times over the years in the higher reaches of the mountain, where the snow cover merges with the cloud obscuring the horizon and making any kind of judgement of scale or distance virtually impossible. We became very used to navigating in such conditions though we never got used to the peculiar effects it produced.

My first experience of this was in the early '50s when a group of us, all keen ski mountaineers, decided to make a circular trip, most of it around the 3,000ft contour on the eastern side of the

Cairngorms. We ran into a blizzard such as I have already described. The disorientation which followed had us all behaving very strangely. What with blowing snow and difficult terrain, each of us became detached from the others and I became convinced I was going downhill far too fast. If I hit anything I couldn't see, then I might be in trouble so I made a stop turn and fell and only then discovered I hadn't been moving at all. It was simply the wind on my face which gave my brain the only piece of information to go on as an impression of movement.

We had many such experiences on Wyvis. On our way up one day, we saw a fox on the lower reaches of the hill and also saw the prints on the snow higher up. So we were ready to encounter a fox anywhere ahead of us. As luck would have it, there was a solid cloud cover above 2,500ft and inevitably we went into the whiteout.

Suddenly, Derek grabbed my arm and whispered, 'Look, the fox, dead ahead.' I peered into the whiteness and sure enough I could see it some distance ahead. It seemed to be in a crouched position as though intent on something just in front of it. Now and then it would move as though it were after a mouse or vole under the snow.

We must have been watching it for a few minutes when Derek said, 'Wow, did you see that pounce?'

'That's funny,' I thought. My fox hadn't moved.

We took a few steps forward only to discover we had been watching a small round stone which had emerged from the snow. Our brains, having seen the fox earlier, were intent on seeing one again.

A more concrete encounter with a fox occurred on a beautiful day in February. Derek and I had separated at the top, he to check wind speeds along the summit ridge while I made a few runs into the corrie, covering as wide an area as possible, to check the snow conditions at various levels. Conditions were marvellous with about six inches of powder snow on top of a solid crystalline base, making skiing effortless and silent. As I went high around the bowl of the corrie, I glanced down to find a fox tripping lightly across the corrie floor – no doubt looking for an unwary ptarmigan or vole under the snow. On turning to make a traverse in the other direction, there was no sign he had spotted me. It was too much of a temptation and I allowed the points of the skis to turn a little more downhill. As the skis gathered speed, there was still no sign that the fox had seen me. He appeared to be intent on something just ahead of him. Just then, the skis scraped across a small patch of frozen snow and the fox leapt high in the air and turned to face me. It was then only about 20 yards away and it made off as fast as the snow would allow but I was gaining very fast. I didn't have the heart to chase it and turned away uphill to allow it to escape. I was rather ashamed; I had given it such a fright.

The Ben supports a large population of ptarmigan and we came across them regularly on every visit. They really are the most incredible bird, seemingly immune to whatever the arctic weather throws at them. Even in the vilest snowstorm, they obstinately refuse to come down from the high tops. So many times we would be struggling against the snow and wind near the top when a ptarmigan would waddle out of the murk, give us a cursory glance then waddle off again intent on reaching an unknown destination. We soon discovered that the most likely place to find them was on the most exposed part of the mountain. Our conclusion was that it was only here that the wind blew the snow cover away enough to expose the vegetation, their staple diet.

They have many enemies of course, one being the fox already mentioned and their best protection is their camouflage. About the same size as the red grouse, the hen bird has a mottled brown appearance in summer while the cock bird is a greyish blue – both with white wings only seen in flight. They blend in perfectly with the broken character of the high tops and prefer to sit still when approached. Over the years, we have taken countless numbers of people on to the tops to look for these birds and it always amused the group when a ptarmigan flies from someone's feet, especially when they are expecting to see one, at best, some few hundred yards away. As winter approaches, so the ptarmigan changes its appearance to suit the conditions, moulting from its summer plumage to a mottled white and brown in early winter to blend with the snow speckled mountain and eventually to a dazzling white in mid-winter.

The golden eagle is their greatest enemy and they keep a constant watch on the sky above, freezing into immobility as soon as the familiar outline appears. It is, of course, an excellent defence, for even the eagle, with its incredible eyesight, cannot pick out the ptarmigan from above against the white vastness of the mountainside. We have on occasion watched the eagle's tactic. It would make an exploratory swoop close to the ground, in the hope that it might startle one bird to panic and fly. Once in the air, it makes an easy target, though once again the eagle has to make a compromise. Too low and it loses the impetus of its swoop whereupon the ptarmigan may escape by making a desperately fast, low flight to shelter beneath a boulder. So it is in the ptarmigan's best interest to fly only as a last resort.

After several winters of survey work, a report was produced by the Ski Development Association which proved that the potential for skiing on the Ben compared favourably with that on Cairngorm. The newly set up Highlands and Islands Development Board showed considerable interest in the work already done and provided some funding for the hire of a tracked vehicle for the next winter in order that we might continue our work and spend more time on the hill, while on occasion taking up interested groups of officials, who were not mountaineers but wanted to see things for themselves. Or at least that was the theory. In practice, it didn't turn out quite as expected, mainly due to our ineptitude in controlling the machine. This tracked vehicle was still in the early development stage of its life. I think they are much more reliable now. It was designed specifically to cover very rough terrain and was reputed to be very good on snow. We spent one day having the controls explained to us and how to tackle various angles of slope, then we were on our own.

Our first attempt to get to the top, we reached a point about halfway when one track hit a hidden sharp boulder, neatly removing one of the tracks. We spent the rest of the day struggling to put it back on and only just got off the hill before dark. On our next attempt, one of the pneumatic tyres around which the tracks revolved developed a puncture and we had to carry the wheel off the hill, have it repaired, then carry it back up to the machine. Once again it was dusk before we got off the hill. Next time it was a fault in the steering mechanism and so it went on. We were spending more time under the machine than on the hill.

On a further occasion we were accompanied by Ian MacKenzie, a Dingwall architect and also a keen skier, with an even keener sense of humour, which was just as well. We were making good progress and beginning to think that this time we would make it to the top. Then once again, on the steepest slope one track came off and we slewed round at an awkward angle. By now we were expert in replacing tracks but on this occasion we had one additional problem; the hand brake wasn't holding as it should and Derek, who was driving at the time, had to remain inside, foot hard on the brake pedal and the engine in gear.

After a hard struggle, Ian and I finally managed to replace the track and Derek was left with the ticklish problem of starting the engine without allowing it to roll back. Ian and I optimistically looked around for large rocks to pile behind the tracks, in the hope that this would prevent such an occurrence, ignoring the fact that the vehicle was designed to overcome such obstacles. At this point, we thought it prudent to unzip the canvas roof from the vehicle so that we might converse with Derek as he prepared to start the engine. We both then leant our weight against the cab, hoping this would give some psychological encouragement, when Derek danced around on the pedals, changing from brake to accelerator and pushing in the clutch as he simultaneously started the engine. As luck would have it, the engine didn't fire first time and Ian and I were thrust aside as the vehicle climbed over our carefully placed boulders and sped off down the hill. We just had a momentary glimpse of Derek's white face as he receded from us. With unerring accuracy, the vehicle headed straight for the burn, leapt off the bank and landed squarely on top of a frozen pool, smashing through the ice, and there it sat with the burn flowing freely through the cab.

Ian and I ran down the hill and shouted, 'Are you all right?'

'Yes, I think so,' he said, seemingly unaware water was swirling around him. Then looking down, he suddenly realised his situation and jumped through the open top out onto the bank with great alacrity. We all stood on the bank and gazed at the vehicle. There was no apparent damage. It was sitting squarely in the burn, wedged neatly between the two banks, with a strong current flowing through it and around it.

'I suppose we ought to try and start it,' I said without much conviction. The others nodded but it appeared hopeless for we thought the ignition system would be under water too. There was nothing else for it but for me to climb through the canvas roof and plunge into the chilling water. Miraculously, the engine burst into life and I was able to edge the dripping vehicle out onto the bank, where Ian made the fatal mistake of opening the door, to be met with a deluge of water which soaked him through. There was nothing left now but for us all to go back down, for we were all soaked to the skin.

A few days later, there was a very heavy snowfall. This time we were determined to reach the top. We chugged our way upwards through the relatively easy route of the Bealach, and then into the foot of the corrie, then upwards toward the summit ridge. Although this route was longer, it avoided most of the very steep slopes. Everything was going well; without effort we passed all the former black spots. It was then the cloud decided to come down and we found ourselves in a whiteout. It was dangerous driving blind in these conditions, so I put the skis on and plodded uphill ahead of the vehicle, with Derek following in bottom gear. Walking uphill on skis is a slow business so the aircooled engine was getting hotter and hotter until finally it stopped altogether and came to a sudden halt. We knew we were high in the corrie but by this time we were not quite sure where. One thing was certain. We had had enough of mechanisation.

'Well, I've had enough of this,' I said. 'I'm going down on ski.'

'Me too,' said Derek. 'We must be very close to the summit ridge so I'll go over the top and glissade down the other side.'

'Good idea. We can meet up at the foot of An Cabar. I'm going down through the corrie,' I said and pushed off down through the greyness. An hour later, we met on the other side and returned to Garbat in silence. That evening I phoned the hirer and told him the whole sad story. He was surprisingly sympathetic and arranged to have a second vehicle and mechanic to meet us at Garbat the next day, so that we might mount a rescue operation. The morning dawned bright and clear. Before leaving home, with a clear view of the Ben, I scanned the top with my telescope and I could see the tiny red dot of the vehicle very close to the skyline. We had almost made it but not quite. I tried to memorise its position in case of another whiteout. The second vehicle had already been offloaded from the lorry by the time we arrived at Garbat and the driver/mechanic was busily strapping a spare engine on to the rescue vehicle.

'What are you going to do with that?' I asked, fearing the reply.

'I thought we would fit a new engine when we find the other one,' he replied nonchalantly.

'You do know it's about 3,500ft up in very deep snow with a very low temperature?' I said

'Oh, that's all right, I'm used to that sort of thing, besides it's much easier than trying to tow it. Can be very dangerous in difficult country,' he said.

I couldn't argue with that but he wasn't dressed for the part, with only a greasy boiler suit under a torn anorak and a pair of smooth soled city shoes to protect his feet. Nevertheless, we bundled into the cab and started up the hill. It was rather pleasant for Derek and I, for there was no need to worry about which angle of slope to tackle nor whether the tension on one track or other was enough to pull it off. We just waved airily in the direction we ought to take and allowed the expert to get on with the technical difficulties of getting us up there.

We had reckoned without the malevolence of the hill towards mechanization, for we had only reached the top end of the Bealach and into the really deep snow, when a sharp boulder hidden beneath the soft snow ripped into the side of the track, puncturing one driving wheel and buckling a vital part of the steering. We all stood looking ruefully at the damage. 'Well, I suppose we'll just have to take the parts off and carry them down for repair,' said the driver. So, yet again we were crawling about on the snow and digging underneath in order to reach various nuts and bolts which were unwilling to be loosened by our freezing fingers. That afternoon saw us staggering down the hill with pieces of machinery clutched in our arms, the driver having the most difficult time with his smooth soled shoes slipping and slithering around the mountainside. By the time we reached Garbat, his feet were frozen and we left him at the nearest hotel to thaw out while we arranged with the local garage to repair the damage. At least we didn't feel quite so bad at our ineptitude, for even the expert was having the same problems.

Next day saw us all once again gathered at Garbat. This time our driver was kitted out with stout wellingtons and we tramped silently up the hill, spare parts strapped on to frame rucksacks. One hour's work and our rescue vehicle was ready to go once more. Our only worry now was that the weather was beginning to close in and as on our original breakdown, by the time we reached the corrie, we were in a whiteout. We were determined not to make the same mistakes again and though I had to walk ahead on occasion, we made sure the engine was switched off until I had made a reconnaissance and returned to the vehicle before proceeding.

On one such stop, it was agreed that we must be very close to the summit ridge and the stranded vehicle. It was pointless using our rescue machine now. We would be much better on foot. Derek made a wide sweep in one direction while I circled the other side. Every two minutes our driver would sound the horn (why they had a horn on something designed for remote roadless terrain, we didn't know). The sound gave us a reference point to head back to. A long continuous blast meant the stranded vehicle had been found. Luckily just as we were thinking of giving up in disgust, the cloud began to lift and soon we could just make out an outline not far from us. At long last, we pulled up alongside the stranded machine. Tools were hauled out and we all set to work on the seized engine. It proved remarkably easy to remove and in the early afternoon the new engine burst into life, very much to our relief, and we made a slow procession down to base once more.

It was getting ridiculous. We had come to the Highlands to escape from all things mechanical and here we were on top of a mountain, up to our eyes in mechanical problems. We decided to stop all this nonsense and return to using ski and foot with a new sense of freedom. How marvellous it was to climb to the top of the hill with no anxiety whatsoever, in the knowledge that we had the reliable use of our own limbs to take us safely back again. We once again began to enjoy our surveys.

The vehicle was used only once more and this time to transport several people from interested bodies to the top of the Ben on a truly remarkably beautiful day in order to see the snow fields for themselves. Notably among them was Sir Robert Grieve, then chairman of the Highland Development Board, who turned out to be an accomplished skier and who decided to make the return trip to the foot of the hill on ski. He made a deep impression on us for there were few chairmen of boards in those days who would be willing to make such a trip, let alone take the unusual step of refusing the easy option of returning in sedate fashion, preferring instead to really enjoy the downhill run.

It may appear from the foregoing that the hill was continually enveloped in cloud but this was certainly not the case. By far the majority of days were spent in sunshine. I have fond memories of sitting on the top in shirt sleeves in January and February, eyes screwed against the glare, gazing over a vast area of Scotland. Ben Wyvis is situated alone, far remote from any other peak of comparable size and consequently commands an uninterrupted view in every direction.

Due south lies the great white mass of the Cairngorms and the Monadliath, further round to the west, the high hills of Glens Affric, Cannich, Farrar, Orrin and Conon. Further round yet, to the west the distant peaks of Torridon – Liathach and Ben Eighe, standing out conspicuously, followed by all the peaks around Loch Maree and Loch Broom, from Slioch and Ben Lair to the awesome Coire Tollan Lochain and the jagged outline of An Tealach and the Fannich hills ending in the lovely conical peak of Sgurr Mor.

To the north and west, the jumble of peaks are a little more difficult to sort out but one can make out the summits of Suilven, Cul Mor, Cul Beag and Ben More Assynt peeping over an intervening ridge of Wyvis. Due north lie the unmistakeable outlines of Ben Hope and Ben Loyal on the Pentland Firth. All the way down the eastern seaboard are the indented fertile coastline of Caithness, Easter Ross, the Black Isle and the Morayshire coast. The blue waters of the Firths standing out against the whiteness of lying snow. A panorama in fact that is difficult to equal anywhere else in Scotland.

On one frosty day with thick snow cover down to sea level, Norma, my wife, and I toiled up the An Cabar ridge, carrying skis. There had been a bit of cloud cover but as we climbed, we emerged above the cloud into beautiful sunshine. It was going to be one of those memorable days, with the clarity of atmosphere described above. We had started early so there was no hurry and we took our time reaching the summit cairn for a leisurely lunch while enjoying the sun and expansive views. It was our intention to enjoy the descent to the maximum for we wanted to ski all the way to Garbat from the south-facing side of the hill. We set off across the corrie in long sweeping leisurely traverses, for the aim was not speed but an attempt to keep running without losing too much height. Near the foot of the corrie we took a traverse, which took us high into the edge of the Bealach and were able to take a diagonal line down to the flat floor of the Bealach. The plan was to try to reach the other end of the Bealach before we came to a halt on the flat. We didn't quite make it but with a short distance using the ski poles, we were running again on the shallow slope leading down to Garbat. An excellent day out.

As time went on, doubts began to be expressed about the wisdom of developing the Scottish hills for skiing. A great number of potentially disastrous mistakes had been made in the development of Cairngorm. With the benefit of hindsight, it is easy to see what ought to have been done but at the time most people were unaware of the direct results of disturbing a sub-arctic environment. Happily, most of the problems have been remedied over the years and I don't hear too much criticism of the existing ski areas nowadays.

In the 1960s, with a natural desire to 'improve' the runs and develop uplift facilities, large tracked vehicles were brought on to the hill and began systematically to bulldoze runs, erect pylons for ski tows and generally change the character of the hill. The result was that slow growing vegetation was removed, natural drainage was upset and bulldozing caused the water to run off the hill much faster, which in turn resulted in erosion as the water dug new channels. The savage scars on the hillside in those early days could be seen from many miles away. To be fair, great efforts were made and are being made to mitigate these problems and a great re-seeding programme was implemented.

However, the experience on Cairngorm caused a great deal of nervousness of this ever being allowed to happen again. So it was that the idea of developing Wyvis lay dormant for several years and then at the end of the 1970s, a booklet was published by John Murray, a headmaster in Bridge of Allan, whose ancestors were from Ross-shire. He had been beavering away quietly and came up with a novel idea that if a rack and pinion railway, such as was in use in the Alps, were used to reach the snow of the Ben, then many of the environmental problems could be eliminated.

The advantages were numerous. A railway of this kind would take up only a tiny strip of land and if a route were taken up the ridges on its southern side, then the water runoff would be minimal. A railway could be constructed from its own track with no damage to the vegetation on either side. On completion it would control access to the hill. People riding to the top could be directed and controlled so that any sensitive or dangerous areas could be avoided. Perhaps most important of all, if the summit were carefully wardened and managed, it could prove a huge attraction for summer visitors to the North West Highlands.

John's idea aroused a great deal of interest locally – both for and against. Very soon a committee representing the businesses of the area was formed to look into the possibilities of how it could be achieved. Three years of argument and discussion produced a report by an independent group of consultants which came out strongly in favour of the scheme, suggesting that with the right government funding, it could prove to be one of the major attractions in the Highlands.

However, the whole scene changed when a new government policy came into force which declared that no new development could be led by local government. So the whole scheme was shelved. John's idea didn't wither though. Someone running the Cairngorm set up had been watching this development idea carefully and a few years later Cairngorm itself had a funicular railway as envisaged by John. I have to say, I was torn in both directions. I really wanted to keep the Ben in winter for myself and there were times I caught myself being annoyed to see someone else on the hill. On the other hand, the area could have produced great skiers if the local children like my own could have had immediate access to the snow on their doorsteps. At any rate these winter explorations of Ben Wyvis were hugely enjoyable in themselves, and in addition they helped see us through the lean winters of the mid 1960s when we were desperately in need of supplementary income.

CHAPTER TEN

Sandwood Bay Magic

SANDWOOD BAY lies some six miles south of Cape Wrath and a combination of factors made the area one of the most popular places for our naturalist groups to visit. In order to reach it, one has to drive from Durness to Rhiconich then westward to Kinlochbervie and take a very rough track for some distance. There is then a walk across a fairly bleak moor which terminates suddenly as one turns a corner and there far below lies the beach, a long curving arc of golden sand, stretching away to the north and terminating at a short cliff some two miles away.

It's only when the walker is on the beach itself that the view to the south is revealed. Standing well clear of the cliff is the tall slender sea stack of Am Buachaille rising to a height of some 250ft. There are no large seabird colonies here, though a number, who prefer the spaciousness of the Sandwood cliffs to the crowded cacophony of Handa and Clo Mor, do nest here. They are mostly Fulmars with a number of Kittiwakes on the Stack itself and several pairs of Shags on the lower part of the cliff. There are a few Auks but they are mostly on passage to either the Clo Mor to the north or Handa to the south. But it's a good place to watch gannets dive into the clear green water of the bay where they can see the swimming shoals of fish against the sandy ocean bed. The birds would come either from St Kilda and other parts of the Western Isles or from Sula Sgeir away to the North West.

Geologically, the bay is very interesting. At its northern end, the exposed short cliff is composed of Lewisian Gneiss and a close look at this formation is well worthwhile. A combination of ice and sea has cut a near vertical wall out of the rock and the pressure planes are clearly revealed. The way the strata has been twisted and folded, as the plastic and molten rock was pushed and pulled into its present shape, some 3,000 million years ago, is truly remarkable. The southern extremity of the beach is composed of slightly younger Torridonian Sandstone. A close look will reveal it was laid down under water, probably in a shallow sea. There are distinct dividing lines where a fine sediment has been deposited by slow moving water, followed by a layer of much larger rounded material laid down and cemented together under much more turbulent conditions. A large and ever changing sand dune system separates the sea from the brackish water of Sandwood Loch where the gulls love to rest and where various waders are to be found. The outlet from this loch to the sea changes from year to year. Winter storms and pounding seas ensure that one outlet is blocked while another is scoured out by the wind.

We were strolling barefoot along the edge of the sea on the first visit of a new season when we noticed something catching the sun ahead of us, on the edge of a newly carved river. Closer investigation revealed that it was part of an alloy propeller blade which had been bent around in an artistic shape. Our curiosity thoroughly aroused, we dug down through the wet sand until we not only exposed the propeller boss but also what looked like the gearbox. It was only then that I recalled a story of how a Spitfire had made a crash landing on the beach near the end of the war. It was in such a remote spot, they could find no way to recover the aeroplane and it had probably written it off. We kept digging to see if we could find any part of the airframe but the combination of an incoming tide and the speed of the river meant that however fast we dug, the trench kept filling with sand and water and we had to give it up. Two weeks later, on my return to Sandwood, what had been revealed had disappeared and I never found any part of it again though I continued to look for years to come.

The bay has always had a reputation for strangeness. Some people claim it has a peculiar atmosphere – perhaps this adds to the fascination of the place. There is an old, ruined cottage within a few hundred yards of the bay overlooking the loch. The last time it was occupied was in 1934 when a shepherd and his family were persuaded to live there and look after the sheep around the bay.

On the very night they moved in, a violent storm blew up out of the northwest. This, coupled with strange noises they had heard in the cottage, made them frightened enough to move out again the very next day.

Then, of course, there is the story of the mermaid which was seen around the turn of the 19th century by a shepherd named Gunn. He claimed that when he was gathering sheep on the edge of the bay, his dog went racing off to investigate something it had seen or sensed among the rocks which lie near the middle of the beach. These rocks are usually cut off at high tide but on the particular occasion, the tide was very low. The dog began to bark at something between the rocks and the shepherd decided he'd better have a look in case a sheep was stranded. When he reached the dog's side, he looked down and saw the tear-stained face of a mermaid. She had evidently fallen asleep on the rocks and awoke to find herself cut off from the sea. Gunn surmised this was the case for he could not converse with her. She seemed not to understand his offer of help. He was also a little afraid for he had heard alarming stories of mermaids and men. In the end, he decided his best course of action was to leave her alone. Soon the tide would be turning and she would be able to return to her normal environment. Needless to say, most people were rather sceptical of his story but Gunn stuck firmly to it, protesting that he hadn't touched a drop for months.

There are stories of ships being wrecked here. Viewed from the seawards side in a storm, it might look as if it were a sheltered bay, for Sandwood Loch would look like an inlet of the sea and a ship might run for shelter. Once beached, the boat would soon be broken up and disappear in the sand. Hence the story of a ghostly sailor that appears to people as they wander through the dunes.

Derek and I were involved in the periphery of one such sighting. We were on the beach with a group who had differing interests and as a consequence, were widely scattered. A few were looking at plant colonies while others were studying the rock formations. Two girls were strolling along the beach when they spotted gannets diving into the clear water and naturally stopped to watch. With binoculars, they could pick out the birds and follow them as they spotted a fish and turned over to make a spectacular dive into the sea. It's an exciting piece of behaviour and they stood rooted to the spot. One of the girls swept her binoculars along the beach as she followed a bird when she found she had passed a peculiar figure standing on the edge of the sea. She left the bird and went back to the figure. He was indeed peculiar and she tugged at her friend's sleeve to draw her attention. He stood there gazing into space. Their description was, very tall, dressed in a striped jersey with seaboots turned down over dark trousers. On his head he had what looked like a tricorn hat and most of his face was hidden by a black beard. They held him in focus for a short time until he disappeared behind a dune.

Strangely, the girls didn't mention what they had seen to anyone, thinking perhaps he was a local eccentric. It was not until the next morning that Derek and I were talking to the girls and they asked if we had seen the strange figure on the beach. We had seen nothing unusual and asked what this person looked like. When we heard the description, we exchanged glances. The girls caught this and guessed there was more to this than met the eye. When we told them they had given the perfect description of the ghostly sailor, they were quite horrified and assured us they had never heard the story of a ghost at Sandwood Bay. It seemed odd to them that a ghost would walk in brilliant sunshine. We, on the other hand, had been visiting this beach regularly for many years and had never seen or felt anything unusual, though we are still hopeful of seeing the mermaid.

The most unusual thing I have seen there was during the week we had a lady who had a pathological fear of snakes. All week, she had been very careful when we stopped on the hill for lunch, to thoroughly inspect the area where she had chosen to sit. When we crossed a moor or an island of deep heather, she would ensure that we crossed it first and had beaten out all the snakes she was certain lurked there. However much we assured her that any snakes that were in the vicinity would most certainly have cleared off at the first sound of our approach and it was a chance in a thousand to actually stand on one and get bitten, she would not be pacified.

On this particular occasion at Sandwood, she came galloping up to me in a great state of agitation, saying she had just seen an adder down at the water's edge. I must say, I was very sceptical, for it seemed a very unlikely place for an adder, for to get there, the snake would have to cross about quarter of a mile of open sand, when I normally expect them to seek cover, as they go about their business. I thought perhaps she had seen a piece of weed washed up by the sea and in her heightened state of aversion, had thought it was an adder. Nevertheless, I suggested we go down to have a close look, but she refused to move from the spot and casting nervous glances all around her, she gave me directions as to how to find it. Much to my surprise, it was an adder and very much alive. Now it was making its way back to the dunes. On my approach, it reared up and we both gazed at each other. Then deciding I was harmless, it continued its progress up the beach. Strange, that of all people to find it, it had to be the person with the greatest fear. She left the Highlands convinced that the whole area was crawling with snakes. Since that incident, I have come across adders on one or two deserted beaches, most often on the Applecross peninsula and can only conclude they are attracted by the sandflies.

Most probably by sheer chance, Sandwood Bay has provided me with the greatest number of sightings of exciting peregrine stoops and kills. During the early years of Highland Safaris, there was a worry that the Peregrine might be wiped out by the indiscriminate use of pesticides but here in the extreme northwest, we were blessed with a goodly number. On one occasion, Derek and I decided to have a look among the cliffs at the southern end of Sandwood for we had, on occasion, seen ring ouzel on earlier visits. It was one of those windless days in June, where the sun beat down from a cloudless sky. The exertions of the climb made it necessary on reaching the crest of cliff to sit down and rest with our backs to the warm rocks. Far below, we could see the other members of our group scattered across the beach, enjoying the day in their own way.

Lazily, we scanned out to sea and across the beach, sometimes drawing the others' attention to a puffin speeding across the water or a skua resting on Sandwood Loch. Then we both picked up a rock dove, winging its way across the beach and heading straight towards us at the same level. When the bird was less than 100 yards from us, a blue shape flashed up into our view from below and hit the rock dove with an almighty blow. We both cried out in surprise, as the dove and the peregrine, for that is what it was, tumbled earthward, locked tightly together. Their downward path carried them out of our sight, beyond the edge of the cliff, whereupon we leapt to our feet and raced to the nearest gully to follow the action. An outcrop of rock still blocked our view but undeterred, we continued to run down the confined space of the gully, hopping from boulder to boulder, in our headlong dash to get a better view. Not surprisingly, our commotion on the descent had frightened the peregrine and we were just in time to see it flash around the edge of the cliff but there at our feet was its victim. It lay on its back, with the head neatly decapitated and lying two feet from the body. It must have been an instantaneous death.

On a second occasion, we were driving very slowly along the extremely rough track which leads to the starting point for the walk to Sandwood. The track twists and turns between a number of shallow lochans and as we approached a small stretch of sandy shore, someone spotted a group of waders resting at the water's edge. Stopping the bus where everyone could see, we concentrated our binoculars on the flock of birds. They were sanderlings, an unusual sighting enough for most of the group to see and we continued to watch in the knowledge that as long as we remained in the vehicle, the birds would be undisturbed. What happened next took only a fraction of a second. One moment, we were watching a group of stationary birds, then suddenly a blur crossed our view, picked up an unlucky individual and zoomed off, while the rest of the flock rather belatedly rose in the air in unison and made off. Fifty yards away, there was the peregrine, sitting on a low rock and already plucking its dead victim.

It would seem unusual for a group of 12 people in a minibus to see such a thing but the same kind of action was seen yet again by another group. We were heading for Sandwood again and were on the road between Rhiconich and Kinlochbervie. The road here follows the coastline of Loch Inchard and is, on occasion, high above on the cliff edge. We usually took this fairly slowly for it was a good place to see great northern divers in full breeding plumage before they headed north to their nesting sites. As we drove along, a gull matched our speed exactly and was gliding at eye level, being only a few yards out from the cliff. Someone asked if it was a common gull. I slowed even further to take a quick glance and confirm that it was indeed a common gull and just at that very moment, the gull was struck hard from behind by the familiar blue shape.

Everyone gasped in astonishment, for had they not had their attention drawn to the gull at that precise instant, they would have missed the kill entirely. We hastily drew into a passing place and everyone leapt out in time to see the peregrine circle above us, its prey tucked under its body and labouring with the weight of such a large kill. After several such wide, circling movements in which its fast beating wings carried it ever higher, it levelled out and made off at high speed, in a long shallow glide, to disappear over the ridge, no doubt to its nest where hungry chicks awaited.

There seems little doubt that Sandwood Bay will remain, for many years to come, one of the more remote and attractive places for those somewhat more active people who love wild, beautiful and unspoilt places. The walk in is not arduous, but once there, the feeling of being totally cut off from the world is complete. This aspect is in itself becoming more and more rare in our crowded country.

I conclude this chapter with a personal story. One day in the 1970s our group was in Sandwood Bay, where we had had a great day out. We were making our way up the long slope from the beach, and I was waiting for the others. An elderly couple passed me and I exchanged a few words with them as they moved down to the shore. I noticed the couple stopped longer and had an animated conversation with Jan Merchant, a fellow Aberdonian and still a very good friend, who was one of our group that day. Jan caught up with me and said, 'How strange to meet that fellow. That was Jim Moir, a technical teacher and former colleague, and his wife.' I was committed to the group and could not head off after the couple. I felt a great sense of guilt, for here was the man who, a quarter a century or more ago, had taken our unruly bank of schoolkids to the Aberdeenshire hills, and had helped shape the direction of my life – a direction which had led to that day at Sandwood Bay. I had walked past not recognising him, as he was not at all as I remembered him. As a 12-year-old I had thought him very tall. Now he seemed only to be about my height – and I am no giant! – and had grown a beard, and it seemed to me, grown old.

I explained the situation to Jan who told me not to worry, and that Jim was still teaching at a secondary school in one of the housing estates in Aberdeen. I resolved to find and visit him on my next winter trip into the city. The school was easy to find and I strolled through the open doors where the janitor directed me down the corridors to the classroom where Jim was teaching a woodwork class. He did not recognise me of course, but I explained who I was, and that I had come to express my gratitude for what he had done all those years ago. I think that he was genuinely pleased that he had helped one young lad all those years back, and we discussed Sandwood Bay and other places we loved. I left feeling good that I had paid my respects, and let him get back to teaching his class.

Writing this I suddenly realised that if I tried to walk into a school today in the way I had back in the 1970s, I could well run the risk of being arrested, such have attitudes changed. However, you can still walk into Sandwood Bay without any such fear.

CHAPTER ELEVEN

Bird Islands: Handa and Mousa

I LOVE ISLANDS – and the business of getting there.

It was always important that we chose the best possible weather to cross to any of the islands in the west and north. There is nothing better than being in a small boat in a flat calm ocean heading for a beach at the beginning of a day which you know the clients will love and remember. Each of the islands were special in their own particular way and it would be difficult to choose which is the best so I have selected two which hold a special place in my memory. The first of these is Handa and the other is Mousa – each totally different from the other in geography but united as a nesting base for different types of seabird. A consequence of my guiding work was that I developed a serious interest in ornithology, partly self-taught and partly supplemented by occasional lessons from clients who, in this area, had specialist knowledge.

For anyone visiting this north-west corner of Scotland, a visit to the Island of Handa is a must, for like Clo Mor on Cape Wrath, it holds one of the largest colonies of seabirds in the area. To get there, one has to travel to Tarbet, one of the numerous Tarbets on the west coast. The name simply means a place of porterage, where boats were hauled across an isthmus to prevent having a potentially dangerous sea journey. In the early 1960s, Alastair Munro was the warden of the island. He was a local fisherman whose only income previously had been from lobster fishing and he had probably jumped at the opportunity to supplement this by transporting visitors across the sound to land on the island. We would phone Alastair first thing on a good, windless morning and say how many people we would be bringing down from Durness, our base for the Sutherland week and he would be waiting for us on the slipway. It was something like a one-and-a-half-mile journey across the sound and sometimes with a larger group and a small boat, it would take one or two trips before everyone was transported across. But it didn't matter for time was of no importance here.

On a good sunny day, the colouring of sea, sky and island is unbelievable. The clarity of the green water meant you could look down onto the ocean bed, with its sandy floor all the way across except on the middle part of the journey where the bed dipped down into darkness. There are two good beaches on the island where one can land, depending on the wind direction and Alastair had a unique landing technique, where he would drive the boat hard up on to the sand, and then an upturned milk crate was thrown in front of the bow onto the shore, and the passengers could land dryshod. The cliffs are on the far side of the island and it is a pleasant one mile, gradually inclined walk which takes one through the abandoned village – now just a group of low, dry stone walls. Like so many other islands in this corner, life in the 19th century was so tough that they were forced to abandon it. Arrangements were made to transport the whole population to a new life in Canada and the story is that a ship hove to just offshore, the islanders were rowed out to the ship with their meagre possessions and were taken directly across the Atlantic to a new life. Desperate times indeed. Finally, the walk ends abruptly at the cliff edge and one is bombarded by the raucous sound of seabirds, gargling guillemots, razorbills, and fulmars, along with kittiwakes screaming their name, 'kittiwake-kittiwake!'.

Only one or two quiet Puffins here, for the best views of these are further on at the Great Stack. The Great Stack is well named for it stands out proud of a V formation on the main 400 foot cliff. The south-east face is literally packed with birds, all sitting on horizontal ledges of conveniently stepped Torridonian Sandstone. One can easily sit and watch the busy traffic from sea to cliff. How they find their own partner and egg on this massive overcrowded, multi-storeyed edifice is a complete mystery.

If one walks round the V on the main cliff, it is possible to get a little closer to the Stack and it is here that most of the puffins reside, near the top, where there is a little vegetation and lots of thrift in flower. The puffins can disappear into small burrows or sit outside and sun themselves. They tend to be much less vocal than their relatives, just quietly getting on with sitting on an egg, or going off to feed when the other of the pair returns. It's when they are feeding the single chick that you may more often see them alight clumsily on the vegetation and you catch the glint of a series of sand eels held firmly in their bills. With serrations on the edge of their colourful bills, they can catch one fish and open their mouth to catch the next one, without losing the first. All the auks are dynamic fliers, where the wing in relation to the body weight means they have to beat the small wing very fast to maintain a forward speed. This creates no problem when alighting on water where only an approximation of the right spot is necessary. When it comes to alighting at a very specific spot on a cliff, it can create immense difficulties. Usually, the auk returning with fish must triangulate its final destination on the cliff from some way out. It already has a very fast forward speed which is difficult to reduce, without falling out of the sky, so the usual technique is to come in low and fast then glide upwards. If it has calculated the approach correctly, it will run out of momentum just as it reaches the right ledge. The evidence of how difficult this manoeuvre can be will be seen where a bird has made a slight miscalculation and it arrives slightly off-kilter. The result, very often, is that it has to go round again or it strikes another bird and several neighbours are all knocked off and they all have to navigate their way back again. Life is never easy.

When we visited Handa in the early 1960s, I noted that there was what looked like a ten-inch diameter wooden post, wedged deeply into a crevice on the top of the Stack. This puzzled me greatly for I knew the Great Stack had never been climbed. I asked Alastair if he knew anything about this and being born and bred here, he told me that amazing story that had been handed down over the years. It is well known that during the seabird nesting season, the men from the Island of Lewis would visit the cliffs of Sula Sgeir and other islands to harvest young gannets, for they were and still are a great delicacy for the islanders. There was great competition among the men as to who were the best climbers and they were always looking for new places to conquer in their quest for more gugas, as they were called.

At the end of the 19th century, three men looked longingly at the Great Stack of Handa for in the season it was teeming with life, but it appeared to be totally inaccessible. Their technique usually involved climbing down from the top rather than climbing up from the foot of the cliff. A boat could quite easily reach the foot of the Stack but it then involved a vertical, very exposed, 400ft climb to reach the top. However, a fellow named MacDonald, who was famous in his day for his climbing abilities thought he might have found a way of doing it.

Armed with great lengths of rope, three men walked across Handa to the Great Stack. The Stack itself sits in a large V away from the main cliff. The idea was that they would anchor one end of the rope at one end of the V and walk around the V paying out the rest of the rope as they walked. Once they were on the other side opposite the Stack, they managed to pull the joined ropes across the top of the Stack and pulling it taut, anchored it on the far side. The distance between the main cliff and the Stack is shorter here and MacDonald pulled himself across this yawning chasm with nothing between him and the sea 400ft below. Naturally, with such an immense length of rope, there was a tremendous amount of stretch and he discovered that when he was halfway across, that he had dipped down a considerable distance. So he had to climb vertically up the rope until he came in contact with the cliff of the Stack and scramble onto the top – an amazing feat of guts and strength.

A re-enactment of this feat was made into a BBC film a year or two back but what happened next was misconstrued by the film-makers. The young climbers were looking from the perspective of the 21st century and thought the Lewismen had done this as a show of bravado and challenge. Nothing could be further from the truth. It was deadly serious for they were looking for reward in gathering a record crop of gugas. Having reached the top of the Stack, MacDonald found a temporary anchor and rigged up a pulley system across the chasm. They had carried with them across the island a sturdy wooden post which MacDonald hauled across and then found a fissure in the centre of the Stack and drove in the post until it was very secure. He could now shorten the rope between the Stack and where the other two men stood which meant they could be hauled across, without too much sag on the short rope.

Once all three were across, they were in their normal environment. They were able to fix ropes to the wooden post and abseil down any side of the Stack, collecting gugas as they went. They had the perfect solution to access the Stack. When they left, they would have secured a doubled rope between the post and an anchor at the nearest side of the main cliff. It was their intention to return the next year and with the doubled rope already in position, it would be no problem getting back on to the Stack. It seems for some reason they never returned. The rope decayed – but the post remained. It was still there in the '60s and I am not quite sure when it finally fell out of its position but probably by the '70s, it had disappeared.

When we first started visiting Handa regularly in the early '60s, there were no skua on the island. A solitary great skua arrived, I think, about 1966 but it seemed to have no idea of what its purpose was in life. Our usual routine was to visit the main cliff colonies then wander up to the summit cairns to eat our packed lunch. From here, one is a little way from the mainland and there is a wonderful panorama of the easily recognised shapes of the Sutherland hills. One can see, starting from the north, Cranstackie, Foinaven, Arcuil, Ben Stack, Canisp, Suilven, Cul Mor, Cul Beag, Stack Pollaidh – and Ben Mor Coigach just outside Ullapool. The great skua would quite happily settle down beside us and feed on a few scraps of meat or fish that we threw to it. But this peace was not to last. Within two or three years, there were quite a number of great skuas who were quite sure what their purpose in life was and it became quite difficult to have any peace at the summit cairn for they had taken it over as part of their territory. Anyone venturing into this area was immediately attacked. They had no scruples about knocking an intrepid individual to the ground by coming in from behind at high speed and giving them a good crack on the head with their lowered feet.

There is a small lochan not far from the summit cairn on Sithean Mor, Handa's high point, where a pair of red throated divers used to nest regularly and it was a great pleasure to watch them from the summit cairn, a safe distance from their nesting site. But one year the skuas had expanded their territory to include the lochan. I could see no sign of the divers nesting early in the year and decided they were not going to nest at all. However, in July, we could see them coming towards the lochan, displaying all the way, whereby they slowed the usually fast beating wings to half speed in unison, holding the wings in a high V shape, and glided in beautiful formation, to land smoothly on the lochan. They were immediately set upon by the skuas who tried to drop on top of them, forcing the unfortunate divers to dive repeatedly until they had to take off and I don't think they ever nested there again.

A walk round the south end of the island takes one past small sandy beaches until the landing beach is reached and a boat waits to bring you back to the mainland. In those early days, there were fewer people visiting the island and Alastair would often take us round below the cliffs for a different view of the colonies. From the sea, the sight looking upwards is even more impressive and it's only here that you realise that the Great Stack is resting on giant legs, for it was possible at certain states of the tide to take a boat right through and out the other side of the Stack.

A summer in these waters gives the impression of being a benign paradise but it can be a treacherous stretch of coastline in winter. In the course of my lifetime, I have personally known no less than five boatmen whose lives have been claimed by the sea.

Their winter occupation of setting out and picking up creels from a tiny, open boat was often hazardous but I hasten to add that if in summer, I were to phone for a crossing when there was even the slightest swell, the men would refuse to take us. Though they might accept the risk to their own lives in winter, they would never, ever, have risked anyone else's life in summer.

A close rival in my affections to Handa was Mousa. Indeed it is difficult to establish a priority there. Both islands always attracted many eager clients for us. Shetland is a magical place for any naturalist. At practically every turn on whichever island there is something to catch the eye from Hermaness and Muckle Flugga in the north to Sumburgh Head in the south. But for my money, the most wonderful experience is to be found on the island of Mousa which lies just off the east side of the South Mainland. For here are found a thriving colony of storm petrels. In the closing years of the 20th century, I would spend some time in the Shetlands with various groups of naturalists and would always try to choose the best possible weather for a visit to Mousa. It is best to visit on one of the longest days of the year in summer when daylight is almost constant, for the storm petrel adults will spend all day fishing far out at sea and only return to feed the chicks late at night and in the early hours for at this time they can avoid the various predators like the skuas.

The most memorable visit I can recall actually looked as though it would not come off for the weather had been very changeable all week but slowly the pressure had been building and the trick was to hold one's nerve until there was some certainty in having a dry clear spell. We had been having our share of sunshine but it was accompanied by a strong westerly wind. It had little effect on our visits to the other islands because the system of ferries connecting each island to the others is so efficient that only severe weather can disrupt them. The only problem being that the breeze made the strength of the sunshine deceptively cool and after a few days of cloudless skies, most people were badly burned. At last the wind finally dropped and Mousa looked possible. I phoned Tom Jamieson who had a small boat based at Sandwick and he agreed that it would probably be possible that night. We had arranged that if we heard nothing from him on our return to the hotel after our day out, the trip would definitely be on for about 11.00pm that night.

The wind had dropped to nothing when we arrived at Sandwick for we seemed now to be right in the centre of the high pressure system. By coincidence it actually was the longest day of the year and the sun was just on the horizon as we slid quietly across the Mousa Sound. To the north, the clear sky shaded from a bright orange where the sun still lurked, through a yellow and pink immediately above us to a deep indigo to the south where a three quarter moon was just rising. No one spoke as we covered the short distance to the island for it seemed it would break the spell. As we slipped into the landing place towards the north end of the island various seals bobbed up from the depths of luminous water and watched curiously as we disembarked. It is perhaps half a mile from the landing place to our destination at the Mousa Broch and as we walked in the gloaming, terns still fished offshore, fulmars glided close by but all was quiet. The atmosphere was such that we spoke in whispers but mostly we were silent only speaking in a hushed tone when we had to warn of some obstacle ahead.

The broch itself is a fascinating structure. Most probably built somewhere between the last century BC and the first century AD, it consists of a circular tapering cooling tower shape about 13 metres high and 15 metres diameter. The drystone structure is built entirely with the flagstone found on the shoreline of the island and is constructed with an inner and outer wall with cells, passages and stairways contained within the two walls leading up to a walkway around the perimeter at the top. It was almost certainly there as a defence of some kind for there is only one entrance and no windows looking outwards. During troubled times it would have been impregnable and it is said there are around 150 brochs to be found around the coastline of the north and west of which Mousa is the most complete. Very little appears to be known of the people who erected these structures but it seems most were used for only a short period, for the need for them appears to have passed by 100AD, though many like Mousa were used by local people right up to the 19th century.

The people who farmed the island all those years ago appeared to be prone to attack by an unknown foe. It would seem that when an enemy boat was sighted, they would drive all the livestock into the lowest enclosure and it is likely there was some kind of flooring above the livestock where the farmers could sit out the attack. The doorway into the broch was deliberately set very low with a guard chamber at right angles to it. If the enemy managed to dislodge the boulder at the entrance, they could easily be dealt with as they crouched to enter. Anyone who was courageous enough to scale the outer wall could easily be pushed off from the walkway around the top of the broch. The wonder is that Mousa Broch is still complete for almost all the other brochs around the North and West have been continuously robbed of good building stone.

Back in the present day, we entered through the low doorway and filed silently inside. Possibly the broch was thatched at one time but now it was exposed to the clear moonlit sky. The atmosphere was almost tangible as one thought of all the generations who had lived and died here. But we were brought sharply out of our reverie by the very sound we had come to hear. Out of the semi darkness came the purring sound of the storm petrel chicks for indeed this was where they nested, between the drystone walls. It's a very strange gentle sound reminiscent of a quiet motor bike engine revving and changing gear. There appeared to be a fairly large number judging by the sound. But still no sign of the adults. Their arrival time can't be depended on for there are so many factors involved. They could be fishing many, many miles out where the weather could be different or they may have to dodge many predators. It was just a case of waiting patiently.

Some time past midnight, someone said they were sure something had just passed his head at high speed and suddenly the petrels were all around flying at suicidal velocity. Looking seawards with binoculars which capture more of the available light, we could see them skimming low over the water, making sudden changes in direction which made it difficult to follow one individual for any length of time. It was a totally silent flight, no wing or vocal sound and they appeared oblivious of our presence. At one point, one bird hurtled past between my neighbour and I who were less than a metre apart. But probably the best view was looking upwards along the edge of the broch where the wall was silhouetted against the sky. We had taken the precaution of carrying torches with us and with the help of these could see these tiny birds, black with white rumps, literally shooting into the wall. There was little evidence of any deceleration. They shot straight into the tiny crevices with unerring accuracy. It was quite remarkable. Only one or two individuals made a mistake and had to sidle along a little way to find their own entrance which gave us the opportunity to have a good look at the outline of the bird, its white rump showing up well in the moonlight.

All this time, the tide had been rising slowly unnoticed but it had risen far enough for Tom to move the boat from the little landing place to a point just under the broch. Very reluctantly, we climbed down the low cliff and filed aboard. Even as we were casting off, birds were still shooting past us at high speed intent on reaching the nest in as short a time as possible. The return trip was just as magical as the outward. The moon, now quite high, threw a shimmering light across the water and two porpoises rolled lazily in the reflected light. We disembarked quietly and drove back to the hotel through a landscape already tinged with the first hint of dawn with small banks of mist hugging the hollows.

The main enemy of the petrels are the skuas. The storm petrel is a tiny bird and no match for the mighty skua, which is probably why the petrels fly back to their nests in semi-darkness. And whilst on the subject of skuas, here would be a good place to narrate a method they have of hunting, which I have observed further north in Shetland, in the Bluemel Sound between Yell and Unst and nowhere else. Here they are mostly great skuas and their chosen victims are very often gannets though the gannet is a much bigger bird than the skua. The gannets nest on the cliffs of Hermaness but fish in the area between Fetlar, Yell and Unst. When they are returning to the nest with fish, they fly through the sound where the great skua are patrolling. These will fly up behind a gannet which is tip to tail 12 inches larger and the skua watches carefully as the gannet flaps, then glides. When the gannet is in the glide position, the skua moves in quickly, grabs the tip of the victim's wing and with a quick upward movement turns the gannet over. Taken by surprise, the gannet usually falls to the sea. Sometimes the gannets give up the catch there and then but a few are determined to hang on to the fish.

The skua lands on the water behind the gannet as it recovers from its unexpected fall and sits there patiently. The gannet makes to take off again and spreads its wings. Immediately the skua springs from the water and lands on the gannet's back pushing the larger bird below the surface. This is repeated again and again until the exhausted bird finally disgorges. We have often had to walk through a great skua nesting colony on Hermaness and I can tell you they do not like any disturbance. They have no hesitation, if you are anywhere near a nest, in attacking you. The usual tactic is for the skua to fly to a height of about 100 feet then dive vertically downwards beating the wings very hard. When they flatten out at head height, they are travelling at something upwards of 60 mph. They come in from behind, drop their feet and hit the unfortunate intruder hard on the head which can send them sprawling. The only defence is for people to watch each other's backs at all times.

CHAPTER TWELVE

Exploring the Far North Coast

WE WERE NOW at a point, by the early 1970s, where we were running almost at full capacity. Most of our clients knew that if they were with us early in the season, it was good for many varieties of birds, having both winter visitors before they leave and summer birds just arriving at one and the same time. Later, the seabirds would come back on to the cliffs and the plants would be good.

We would often spend a day or two exploring the North Sutherland coastline, which was in itself very varied and interesting. We would stop and have a walk at the sea edge to the south of Port nan Con which is on the western edge of Loch Eriboll. This was geologically a good place to find one of the first visible signs of life on the planet. The oldest rock in the north-west is Lewisian gneiss whose dates the geologists keep pushing back. Last time I heard, they thought it to be 3,000 million years old. On top of the gneiss is a deep layer of Torridonian Sandstone of which the mountains of the north-west are composed. Finally, there is a cap of Quartzite and it's here that the first signs of life appear for these last two layers were laid down under a shallow sea.

Instead of taking everyone to the top of a hill to examine these, we could look at them here at Port nan Con. For on the east side of Loch Eriboll there had been a great earth movement which heaved everything violently to the west, turning all the rock layers upside down. This is named the Moine Thrust after the great moor on the east side of the loch. The quartzite was crushed down and a lot of it shattered. By strolling along the shore line everyone could pick up a number of small rocks, which showed in cross section the worm casts of ancient life on the sea floor some 600 million years back.

In the 1960s there were still a few fishing boats which would call in here to unload their catch or to make a small repair. Though the pier was slowly disintegrating it was still serviceable. On this particular occasion, I had a large group of Flemish Belgians, who were all keen naturalists, and among their number was a priest who had a great sense of humour and spoke very good English. He was, of course, out of uniform. It so happened that there was a fishing boat tied up at the pier and being very curious, the priest went across to speak to the crew. Evidently they had had a minor breakdown and a crew member had been sent off to find a new piece of equipment. Seeing the priest's interest, they invited him aboard and showed him around, completely unaware of the nature of his calling. One or two of our group struck up a conversation with other members of the crew and while doing so, they spoke of their fondness for the priest. The crew were aghast, they were East Coasters and VERY superstitious. A minister on a boat was an exceedingly bad sign.

I was completely unaware of what was going on when a member of the crew gave me a good telling off for allowing such a thing to happen. I thought the superstitious nature of sailors had died out long ago – but not so. When I arrived a couple of weeks later, the same boat was there again unloading, and the skipper made a bee-line for me and said, 'I told you so. We went out the same day and caught a rope round our prop. Are you sure there are no men of the cloth with you this time?' I of course re-assured him but couldn't believe he was serious. That same week with the Flemish group, we were looking at the boats at the pier in Kinlochbervie when, would you believe, a fishing boat was coming alongside and a crewman threw a rope saying: 'Catch this will you.'

Guess who caught it. The crewmen were puzzled by the gales of laughter as the priest turned to us, grinning while tying the rope to a bollard.

Leaving Loch Eriboll, one goes over the hill and descends to Loch Hope. We would often spend a day down there, for if the group were fit enough, we would climb Ben Hope, Scotland's most northerly Munro. It's a fairly straightforward climb. The lower part, we discovered, was a very good place for sightings of adders. They would sun themselves on the rocks by the burn which drains part of the Ben. If the weather was not with us, we would wander down the river which flows into the loch. It was often good for sighting goosanders or mergansers and quite often we would see black throated divers in the Loch. There was a remote house on the other side of the river which could only be reached by crossing a deep ford but it had a rope and pulley contraption on top of a post on each side. We often wondered what its purpose was. Then one day, our arrival coincided with the postman. He pulled one end of the rope and placed the post in a pouch then pulled the other end of the rope and the mail whizzed to the other end. He then shouted, 'Dolly!' and Dolly duly came out of the house and collected her mail. An ingenious device.

The narrow road east crosses the great moor of the Moine and then down to the shores of the Kyle of Tongue. When the tide is right, it's a great place for common and grey seals lying out on the sandbanks. It's also a good place for greenshank and other wading birds. There are a series of small islands where the road comes down to the edge of the Kyle. This used to be a great place for the nesting Common and Arctic terns and there is a grassy bank just outside the cemetery, where we would sit and watch their comings and goings, easily recognisable with their ever buoyant flight, carrying sand eels to their chicks on the safe islands. However, a road widening scheme meant that rather than follow the old route round the inner end of the Kyle, the new route to the village of Tongue now crosses the islands, cutting off a long detour. As expected, the terns disappeared from the islands over the course of the next few years but we continued to use the old route which was much more interesting and takes one closer to Ben Loyal.

This would normally be the furthest extent of our journey east-wards, for beyond this point the terrain gradually changes from one of wildness to a more tamed landscape. It was towards the end of the season in 1972. The seabirds had already gone, most of the chicks were off the nest and it was a generally quieter time of the year. I had heard of the island of Eilean na Ron, just out from Skerray, further east of Tongue which had been abandoned just before the start of the Second World War. It was a familiar story of the islanders having lost a lot of their man power as people drifted away, reaching a point where it was no longer viable as a community. Subsequently the whole population moved on to the mainland, leaving the island and its houses empty. I had also heard that it was a good place to find grey seals in the breeding season, so I thought it a good opportunity to do something different by visiting a new island, which could be very interesting. If it looked good, I would come back when the grey seals were on the beaches on a second exploratory visit.

Asking around, I discovered that the only person who was still regularly fishing in the area was Hector MacKay so I duly phoned him and arranged for my group to be taken out to the island the following day. It was quite an ancient boat but a solid one, with one of those very noisy diesel engines which had such a heavy knock that it was difficult to converse. As we sailed slowly around the island's coastline, we could see the houses of the village and to our great surprise, there was smoke coming out of the chimney of one of the houses. From the bow, I shouted back to Hector, 'So there's someone living on the island now, I see!'. He nodded but obviously didn't hear exactly what was said. It was only when he had killed the engine as we came into the landing stage with steep concrete steps leading up to the cliff top that he was able to tell us some of the story.

This was the time of flower power, love and peace; the hippie era. A group of hippies had set up camp on the Rabbit Islands at the mouth of the Kyle of Tongue but it became quite obvious very soon there was no way they could sustain any kind of community here. They too had heard the story of an abandoned island to the east with houses they thought they could inhabit again. It's true that some of the houses still had reasonably good roofs. So they had moved en masse across to Eilean na Ron with the one boat they possessed. The local authorities were quite worried about this development, for there were several very young children with the group and one newly born baby. Hector heard that the health department had been trying hard to get them off the island again before there were any health problems with the children.

So with this new knowledge we clambered up the steps to the top of the cliff. By this time, we were ready for lunch and we all settled down in a wide circle on the heather and unwrapped our sandwiches made up earlier by the hotel. We were chatting away when someone said in a low voice, 'There is someone observing us from behind a boulder over there.'

Of course we all turned to look and realising he had been seen, this bearded, ragged character came out from behind along with a very thin collie to which he hung on to very tightly. We tried to strike up a conversation asking how long he had been on the island and how many there were. He was very vague saying there were a number of them and they hoped to start a new life here. All the time both he and the collie were eyeing up the sandwiches, some of which were lying on the heather beside their owner. Suddenly, the collie could stand it no longer, wrestled free of its owner, darted in, seized a sandwich in its jaws and made off, pursued by the bearded man. We watched in amazement as the man threw himself on top of the dog and wrested the sandwich from its slavering mouth and walked back to return it to its owner with an apology. Not surprisingly the owner of the sandwich said, 'Oh no, you're very welcome to have it.'

At which the man tore the sandwich in half, threw one part to the dog and ate the other half ravenously. How they hoped to survive a winter there we couldn't imagine.

Lunch over, we proceeded to wander around the coastline looking at the various pebble beaches for possible grey seal birthing and mating sites. We kept a distance from the old village but could see the new arrivals had attempted to make a few repairs to two houses and render them watertight. Smoke was emerging from the chimneys but it was obvious they were cannibalising pieces of wood from the other houses. At one point, they had tried to cut some peat and stack it. They had not realised there is an art in peat cutting and stacking. The peat is usually cut in spring and stacked in such a way as to run the rainwater off of the stack – rather like roof tiles. We could see their stacks would never dry for they had only recently cut the peat and stacked it badly, allowing rainwater to soak in to the centre.

At last it was time to leave and we could see Hector chugging across from Skerray to pick us up. Naturally we were full of what we had seen and the return journey's conversation consisted of how long the hippies would stick it out. Hector was sure the first winter gale would see them making a full retreat because there was no way they could sustain themselves over a full winter. One month or so later at the end of the season, I phoned Hector again to see if he would take Norma and I across to the island once more to see if there was any seal activity. He readily agreed and I asked him about the hippie commune. He said, 'Oh, they're all gone.' The health authorities had found a legal way of getting them off the island because of the children being at risk. So Norma and I arrived at Skerray and joined Hector on his fishing boat and chugged across to Eilean na Ron once more.

We were only there for the day and had arrived early. We could not have chosen better for there were perfect blue skies and almost no wind so it was an easy saunter around the edge, if a little disappointing that there was not yet much activity among the seals. We sat down on a headland and opened our picnic lunch and ate while scanning with binoculars. Norma gave me a nudge, 'There's someone on that headland over there.'

I twisted round. Sure enough we could see a figure walking towards us. We thought perhaps it was someone who had their own boat and had arrived on the island sometime after we did.

'Hello,' we said. 'Just arrived?'

'Oh no, I'm living here,' he said.

'How long have you been here?'

'I came here with a group from the Rabbit Islands a couple of months ago,' he said

'We thought they had all left.'

'Well, they did but I decided to stay.'

'We didn't see a boat,' we said

'I haven't got a boat. We only had one and they took it with them,' he said.

'But how do you get supplies.'

'I don't. I've caught some fish and I'm drying a lot of them in an open ended sea cave.' It was certainly true that the former islanders had dried their fish in this same cave as there was a perpetual wind blowing through it. Norwegians did much the same thing.

We had a large flask and Norma said, 'Would you like some coffee?'

'I would love some. I have a little tea left but nothing else.' It was obvious that he was living on almost next to nothing and we offered him whatever else we had in the rucksack, which he gratefully accepted. We then strolled with him back to the house. I was curious to know what repairs he had made to the house to make it habitable. He led us to a building where the roof looked reasonable and took us through the front door and then into an inky black room. He apologised for this and said he would let some light in and proceeded to remove a corrugated sheet from the glass free window. The state of squalor was then revealed. As a youthful mountaineer I was used to living in bothies in remote parts of the highlands, but even we survived in better conditions than this.

The room was strung with pieces of rope from which were suspended long lines of wet clothing and wet socks. A bucket of water lay in the centre of the room from which his cat was drinking. There were various cooking utensils scattered around the floor near his grubby sleeping bag, which hadn't been cleaned for some considerable time. The fireplace didn't look as if it had been in use for some time and he admitted that he restricted himself to a fire only in the evenings, for as we well knew the peat stack was still sodden and he wanted to ration the wood he salvaged from the other houses. He offered us some tea and made as if to light a fire but we hastily declined, noting the filthy billy can and that his only water was that from which the cat also drank. 'Don't you think you ought to come off the island with us?' we said. 'It's unlikely that Hector will be back to the island again this winter.'

'No, no,' he said 'I'll be fine. I just have to sort things out a bit and make the house more comfortable.' He had no inkling of what a winter could be like on the north coast of Scotland and was still under the impression that the peat stack would dry out and he could live off the land and sea without a boat. He had this romantic idea of self-sufficiency which was completely unrealistic and we could not persuade him otherwise. We said we would have to go, as Hector would be collecting us soon, and he decided to walk back with us to the landing stage. We could see the look of shock on Hector's face when he came alongside. He did not expect to find a third person there. We explained the situation and Hector too tried to persuade the young man to leave with us, but he steadfastly declined. Hector finally said, 'Well, if we can't persuade you, is there anything we can do for you before we leave?'

'Well, there is one thing. The others left a week or so back and before they left they sank a large wooden box with live crabs out from the shore. You can see it marked with a buoy. Could you pull it up and take it back to me? That should be a good supply of food for a few days.' Hector started the noisy engine and with us aboard chugged out to the buoy saying, 'This is a waste of time. The crabs will have gone cannibal by this time.' We hauled up the box which was well punctured with holes cut to allow the seawater to flow through, took it back to the shore and handed it over to the young lad. After a last futile attempt to persuade him to come with us, we left him and returned to Skerray. It was my full intention to contact Hector at the beginning of the next season to discover what had happened to the young lad over the winter. But tragically, when I opened the local paper in March of the following year, I discovered that both Hector and his friend John Anderson had been lost at sea while on a fishing trip. So I never discovered how the young lad had fared.

Starting a new life in the Highlands might seem idyllic to many – and it had done to this young lad. But it is a difficult place to make a living and the winters are testing. You cannot just wander there and hope things work out. I was fortunate, I had a definite plan and the skills and experience to back it up, as well as personal support from my business- and life-partners. The lad had nothing. No skills, no experience.

Nothing but dreams.

CHAPTER THIRTEEN

Skye Highs over the Years

OUR GUIDING gradually took us to places that were remote, including the Isle of Skye. Not a place back then that had hundreds of thousands of visitors and an all year round tourist trade. I never thought when I went there as a young man in the 1950s, that a decade or so later, I would be leading and guiding others on the Misty Isle. Before I deal with that, let me first narrate a tale which shows as much as anything how the Highlands and access to them has changed over the last 50–60 years.

We climbers and walkers are incredibly fortunate to live in a country where, from about every centre of population, we can be in wild and mountainous areas within an hour or two, have a full day on the hill and be home in the evening. This is almost entirely due to the ownership, or access to, some kind of personal transport. Were it not for the motor vehicle, very few of us could be Munro-baggers for example. Even with the rise in free time available to most people, reaching some of the more remote peaks would prove much more of a problem and a challenge.

The story I am about to tell, of trying to reach what at that time, in the 1950s, were remote areas, is by no means unique. Almost everyone who was climbing then will have a similar story to tell, for we were all limited by the same lack of transport, cash and time. We were, however, always keen to expand our horizons and would go to almost any lengths to explore a new area. So it was that Stan Gordon and I found ourselves very unusually with a week's holiday in the spring. I seem to remember we had to work over the summer trades week in Aberdeen and were given a week in spring to compensate. Our home patch was, of course, the Cairngorms, for there was a decent public transport system from the city to upper Deeside. But we had heard great stories of how good the climbing was on the Cuillin Ridge of Skye and were determined to get there if at all possible.

The venture had to be done on a shoestring and we spent hours planning how we could cut corners and cost to make the whole thing possible. The obvious way to save money as youngsters was to hitchhike but this would take an unknown length of time, so we decided to compromise by taking the train one way to Inverness and hitching from there. We envisaged another problem in this. We would be carrying an enormous amount of gear, in the form of food for a week, tent, ropes and boots. We were still climbing in tricounis at that time so always tried to save the nails by walking in baseball boots and only donning the nailed boots when we were actually on the hill. Would anyone want to pick us up with all this gear? Could we even carry it all? Stan came up with a brilliant idea. We would find ourselves a large, sturdy box and fill it with all the heavy equipment and food, then post it to ourselves c/o the Post Office at Glen Brittle on Skye. So at little cost that problem was solved. We just had to carry the bare minimum to see us through to Skye.

We still had to work on the Saturday morning prior to the holiday, so it was late afternoon by the time we came off the train in Inverness, but we managed to secure a lift to Garve, where we decided to camp. Every road west and north from there was still single track at that time and we hadn't taken into account that the next day was Sunday, with no commercial traffic feeding the various villages. There was practically no tourist traffic at that time, so we only succeeded in getting as far as Stromeferry on Loch Carron and had to camp there until the ferry started again early on the Monday morning. This turned out to be a great advantage for it meant that everyone had to stop there, so securing a lift to Kyle of Lochalsh was easy, as it was again at the ferry from Kyle to Skye, and by mid-afternoon we were at Sligachan. That was exactly where we wanted to be, for we had a nugget of information which would help us on our way, given to us on one of our homeward journeys from Braemar to Aberdeen by a fellow traveller on the Strachan's bus at the end of a weekend.

This journey home to Aberdeen on a Sunday evening after a weekend of climbing was never wasted, for it was a mine of information. We would all exchange experiences of what had happened to each small group during the period. Some may have gone into an area where you had never been; others would have had an encounter with an angry keeper, found a new route, come onto the bus at an unexpected place or been to a bothy that you hadn't yet visited. Everyone was interrogated and the information filed away for future use. I suppose it was an early form of the internet. Someone had been to Glen Brittle at some point and he advised that we should try to be on the road between Sligachan and Glen Brittle in the late afternoon, for there was a contractor who lived there and he invariably came home either from Portree or Broadford in his lorry at the end of a working day and would pick up any climber who happened to be on the road.

The information was spot on. The lorry stopped, we clambered aboard and were off at high speed. The only drawback was that at that time the Glen Brittle road was tarmac for only a short distance, but the contractor didn't slacken speed when he hit the pot holes so we were bounced all the way to his house, just short of the bay. It didn't matter. We were exactly where we hoped to be on the Monday evening and we strolled down to the bay to choose our camping place for the next three days. Being early evening, the Post Office was closed, so we spent that beautiful April evening eating what we had left with us and gazing upward in anticipation to the jagged outline of the Cuillins. There was not another soul in sight.

What surprises me now is that I can recall no anxiety or worry that our parcel may not have arrived as we strolled down to the Post Office the next morning. Perhaps it was the naivety of youth or just a blind faith in our public services in those times. We had every expectation it would be there, and it was. I doubt if I would have had the same confidence today. So began three days of perfect weather and climbing. We were not tigers. We would just enjoy doing as many of the classic climbs as we could fit in. As we pulled on our boots, we discussed where we should start and agreed the first one should be the Cioch Direct, for we had seen spectacular photographs of this airy perch halfway up the face. It was everything we had hoped it would be. Next on the list was Mallory's Slab and Groove, and so on. Many of the names of the climbs we did escape me now, since it was 60 years ago, but it was a very happy time. We ended every climb eventually on the ridge and it became more and more difficult to drag ourselves away at the end of each day, for the weather was crystal clear and the views to the peaks of Rum and the Sgurr of Eigg and round to the mainland were truly spectacular, to say nothing of gazing down to the dark waters of Coruisk at our feet.

Here I have to make a full and frank confession. We ended each day by running down the Great Stone Shoot. There – I've said it and, yes, I can almost hear the gasp of horror: 'Who are those people? Don't they realise there are things you should not do on the hill?'. Our only defence is that there were no rules then. There were so few people on the hill it didn't occur to anyone that this might cause such destructive erosion over the years, that the top of the stone shoot would recede further and further downhill. It was only later, when more and more people had the leisure time to spend on the hill that it became so obvious this was a very bad habit. So I can only apologise to everyone for our part in this. It won't happen again. In fact, we only met two other people in those three days of climbing and they happened to be arriving at the Cioch just as we were about to leave. They told us there were one or two climbers at the Youth Hostel but we were the only other people they had met too. So we joked a little about that old chestnut that when you need a belay in the Cuillins you just hook your woollen jersey onto the gabbro and you are secure. But it was true that the fingertips become quite worn with the rough nature of the rock.

Very reluctantly we had to think about planning our journey home. It was an unwritten law amongst our crowd that if you found yourself west of the Cairngorms then you had to return home to Aberdeen via one of the hill passes. Usually it was either through Glen Feshie or by the Lairig Ghru. We decided on the Lairig. This time we would have to carry all our gear with us, for we might be in need of it. Our friend with the lorry left for work at some ungodly hour in the morning so on the Friday morning we walked out via the Bealach a' Mhaim to Sligachan. From there to the Cairngorms is now a complete blank in my memory. Hitching was only a means to an end so it was of no importance.

My memory comes back into sharp focus again on the Saturday afternoon. We were each hunkered down behind a scots pine near the edge of the tree-line and the entrance of the Lairig Ghru. A wind was roaring out from the mouth of the pass, carrying with it horizontal sleet and snow. We were optimistically hoping that, if we waited long enough, the severe conditions would abate somewhat, for we knew what awaited us at the top of the pass. The time factor was beginning to play a part. We had to be on the 7.00pm bus to Aberdeen on Sunday and would be in trouble at work if we were not. It was no good waiting. We had to face the fact that we had to go on regardless. Bent almost double against the wind and wet snow, we struggled upwards towards the summit of the path. It's worth saying a word or two about rain gear at this time. Everyone seemed to have had a different idea back then of how one should keep dry on these occasions. Some swore by those dreadful army rain-capes, but they were so voluminous that in a strong wind you could almost be carried away. Others went to the extreme of dipping their anorak in linseed oil and letting it soak until saturated, but it never seemed to completely dry out again and the smell remained forever. Most of us chose the middle way, which was to soak the anorak in a solution of alum and warm water. This did give a degree of waterproofing but in relentless weather you were eventually soaked regardless.

It was now heavy, persistent, wet snow driven by a gale-force wind at the summit and we were sodden. We had hoped to get as far as Bob Scott's bothy at Luibeg that evening, which would give us an easy day on Sunday, so we struggled on. But eventually the idea was beginning to form in our minds that we would be forced to call it a day at Corrour. There was no conversation between us by then. We stopped momentarily, faced each other, and said 'Corrour' before struggling onward. For those unfamiliar with the Lairig Ghru, Corrour Bothy is situated directly under the Devil's Point and, although very basic at that time, it has been a lifesaver for many a climber and walker caught by the vagaries of weather halfway through the pass. There was a rope bridge across the Dee to the bothy then: the bottom rope for your feet and the other at chest height for the hands. We clumsily crossed this, arms and legs frozen, and fell thankfully through the door of the bothy.

Corrour in the 1950s was the most spartan of all the bothies. At that time there were four walls, a bench, a half-decent roof, a beaten earth floor and a fireplace in which I had never seen a fire because there was nothing to burn. As I've mentioned before, others spoke airily of digging up tree roots of the Old Caledonian Forest and burning these, but any bog timber of this nature we found on former visits was always so wet it would have taken months to dry out. So we were resigned to taking off our sodden clothing and digging into our rucksacks for our spare gear. Thank goodness for ex-army frame rucksacks. They had a rubberised lining on the inside which kept everything dry and we were soon inside our sleeping bags, dry at last, with the primus brewing up some soup.

Our climbing rope is perhaps worth a mention here. It was in the days before nylon and we were climbing with Indian hemp, which was fine when it was dry. But when the fibres were wet they swelled and the rope became very stiff and unmanageable, so any wet climb would take so much longer because we had to struggle with the rope. On this occasion it came off the top of my rucksack shaped like a modern bronze sculpture and remained in that shape until we got home.

We awoke the next morning to a complete silence. The wind had dropped overnight and a glance outside revealed bright sun and a scuffing of snow on the ground. This was a great relief for it would be unnecessary for us to put back on our sodden clothes.

We would take a chance on it keeping dry until we got to Braemar. The walk back was uneventful and we boarded the familiar bus on the Sunday evening. It was now our turn to be interrogated.

'If you're hitching,' we said, 'Try to be beyond Sligachan by late afternoon. There's this man with a lorry...'

Leaping forward a decade, from the 1960s onwards, we ran a week on Skye which was very popular. By this time, a road had been pushed through the south side of Loch Carron which cut out the need for the ferry at Strome. (Though this road too has its problems in winter with rock falls.) This had the effect of cutting the journey time by the north route to Kyle of Lochalsh by a considerable margin. If I remember correctly, we were still using turntable ferries at this time as we were also doing at Kylesku and Ballachullish.

Our business was developing well as word spread among the amateur naturalist community. It particularly appealed to single women who were very keen naturalists but were wary of going into quite remote areas by themselves. This way they could be with a group who had the same inclinations, make many new friends and walk confidently in the most difficult of areas, with the knowledge that at the end of each day they would be back in a decent hotel for a good meal and could relax in friendly company. Our base then on Skye was the family run business of the Cuillin Hills Hotel which faces south over the bay of Portree to the Black Cuillin to the south and an excellent centre for reaching every part of the island.

Our strategy as on every week was to watch the weather forecast closely on the previous evening. It was usually possible to plan the day to suit the weather, so we never revealed where we were going until the day dawned and we saw whether the weather on the ground was as predicted. This worked well on the mainland where we could dodge from coast to coast to suit the weather, it being often quite different on each coast. So if for example a front was approaching the Outer Isles in the afternoon, we would dash across to the western lochs. There we would manage a full morning looking for great northern divers, mergansers and eider along with waders and then after lunch would retreat to a fairly high position on the eastern side of the Black Cuillin where we could look for eagles and have a clear view to the west. As soon as we saw the Outer Isles disappear under the approaching cloud, we would get as far east as possible. Usually you had about two hours before the rain reached your position. Of course, it didn't always work. A front would come in slower or faster but in the main we were able to work the weather to our advantage whether we were in Shetland, Ross or Sutherland. I have to say, the Outer Isles were trickier for it was difficult to estimate how far out in the Atlantic the leading edge of the front would be. We tried to off-set this by always being on those islands in the early spring when the weather was rather more reliable, but even then we could dodge around the islands and it's remarkable how sheltered some areas can be.

Very often we would work this in reverse. The forecast would say rain in the morning, clearing from the west. On days like this we would take our time travelling through the rain and be on the west ready for the first glimmer of dry weather. Our clients soon became used to our reticence in saying where we were going the next day and it became a standing joke that someone would try to squeeze the plan out of us for the next day, but we learned early on never to reveal our thinking. On that climbing week in the 1950s discussed above, we were extremely fortunate with weather, where every day was crystal clear and cloudless. Had it been a bad week, we would have been stuck in Glen Brittle and probably soaked every day and the climbing would have been miserable. We would have climbed regardless for we thought it unlikely we would be back for some considerable time. Better roads and reliable transport meant we could dodge around the island and make the most of it.

Most of our clients had a specific interest whether it be ornithology, botany, geology etc but they all enjoyed a bit of adventure so on one day of the week we would visit the north end of the island and get on to the Quiriang, via the very narrow single track road which leads over to Uig. We would park at the highest point (there was never anyone else there in those days) and explain what we hoped to do which was to cross below the cliff, climb beyond the Needle and make our way into the Prison where one is totally enclosed by cliff and a green sward. It was a very secret place then. Sad to say, no longer a secret. A few of the clients were perhaps a little dubious about their ability to get there, but I always made the point they could turn back if they thought it beyond them, for I knew that when we reached the Needle, those who were a little more fainthearted would immediately realise their limitations. Those who continued thoroughly enjoyed the scramble and loved being totally enclosed in that enchanting place.

Also at the north end of Skye lies that other piece of volcanic rock which must be visited. The Old Man of Storr, a vertical column of rock which is probably the plug for an ancient volcano. It appears that a landslip, one of the largest in Britain, had torn the side of the volcano away leaving the plug and one sidewall of the volcano behind. It's not too difficult to reach and was a favourite climb for our clients. The Old Man of Storr is probably the most recognised landmark on Skye and we would spend a morning or afternoon walking up to its base. My chief memory of the area at that time is that it was crawling with rabbits, consequently there were usually lots of buzzards and the occasional eagle. In the early part of spring, it was always a good place to find ring ouzels, the mountain blackbird which looks like an ordinary blackbird, but with a distinctive crescent on its chest. We would walk a little way into the corrie behind the Old Man and if I whistled a monotonous four note call, almost always, a ring ouzel would pop up to see who was invading his territory. Once again, sadly, it's a bird I don't often see now. But back then it was a very dependable sighting.

The Old Man is one of the few places I have had a moment of botanic glory. My inability to retain any knowledge of flowers from one year to the next was the source of great leg pulling from the much more knowledgeable members of the group. By the end of one season, I would have a fairly good knowledge but by the beginning of the next it would all have gone and I would have to start all over again. One year I had a number of good botanists with me on Skye and the holy grail on that early week was seeking out the purple saxifrage which flowers on mountains in April to May. We had searched everywhere but not come across one in flower all week. It was the last day and we had decided to have one final try on the Old Man. First thing in the morning, we looked out to find it had snowed overnight and the group had resigned themselves to having missed that particular plant on Skye, but ever optimistic, we decided to do the climb anyway for this viewpoint since it would be quite different under snow. It was a forlorn hope but perhaps there might be a quick thaw at this time of the year, I hoped.

Alas, when we arrived at the Old Man, the snow was as deep as ever. As the others sat down to gaze over to Raasay, I decided to look around the base of the Old Man because I thought I might be able to remember where we saw the elusive flower the previous year. My memory for place is better than my memory for plants and I carefully scraped the snow away. Lo and behold, there was the purple saxifrage in full flower. I became an instant hero, but I am sorry to say, it didn't ever happen again.

Almost always, the highlight of the week was a trip into Loch Coruisk. There were several lobster fishermen with small boats based in Elgol at this time and we thought they would be only too keen to take our groups into Coruisk. As for the rest of Skye, it had an incredibly long coastline and high attractive hills where we would have no difficulty in finding lots of wildlife. There was one problem, though. In every part of Ross-shire and Sutherland, we had been welcomed with open arms by all the boatmen who were only too pleased to supplement their income by taking our groups to any island we chose. In the 1960s, this didn't seem to be the case at Elgol. We needed a boat to take us from Elgol up the length of Loch Scavaig, to a point where we could disembark and then walk into Coruisk. The boatmen most probably had their own good reasons but they seemed very reluctant to take us to Coruisk and if they did, they would land us on a quite difficult spot and only allow us less than one hour to get to the loch edge and back. This of course was not what we wanted. We needed to spend at least several hours to explore. We knew that there was a landing stage further round the coastline which was erected in Victorian times for steamers to pay a visit to this dramatic landscape and, though it was now rusted, it was certainly sturdy enough to scramble up. The boatmen were just unwilling to spend an extra five minutes to get there and allow us more time at Coruisk.

It got to the ridiculous stage where we would arrive at Elgol and I would immediately scan the slipway below to see where the boatmen were. If they had already seen us, the area became deserted. If I saw one of them before he saw me, I would dash down to the shoreline and try and catch him before he made off. If he was quick, he would jump into the boat, start the motor and take the boat just far enough out so that a conversation was impossible. It was galling, for they did not see they were sitting on a veritable gold mine. Every visitor to Skye would love to get into Coruisk and if they had set it up properly and organised it between themselves, they could have made a very good living. The trouble was, if you couldn't get in by sea, it meant a seven-mile walk each way from Kilmarie on the road to Elgol to get in. This also meant getting across the Bad Step, a sloping piece of rock which if you misjudged it, could send you slipping and sliding into the sea. All in all, it looked like we may have to give one of the best and spectacular parts of Skye a miss.

Then, we were saved. Donald MacKinnon, I think, had been born in Elgol but his parents had emigrated to New Zealand when he was very young, but he had returned as a young married man and had seen the tremendous untapped potential of taking people up into Coruisk. He had the good sense to invest in a really good boat and at last the pressure was taken off me. All I had to do was to wait for a good forecast the night before and give Donald a ring. We would fix up a time which was suitable for him and we would go straight down to Elgol where he would be waiting and then be whisked up to the rusted ladder at Coruisk where we would disembark and he would return to Elgol to pick up the first passengers of the day while we spent the best part of the day at Coruisk.

It's an amazing place. It's composed of great boiler plates of Gabbro, a volcanic rock, and indeed you are more or less in the middle of an ancient volcano which was last active some 55 million years ago. There is a great circle of jagged peaks piercing the skyline around you which had been the crater edge now weathered into great spires of rock. The glacier of the last ice age had forced its way out through the mouth and into the sea where you now land. It can be a forbidding place without sun for the rock is black and doesn't reflect light but even here one can find lots of plant life and in early summer, both common and arctic terns use the islands on Loch Coruisk as a safe place to nest. What could be better than to lie on a warm piece of gabbro and watch the screaming terns fly overhead in that remarkable buoyant flight each with a fish in its mouth for the young on the island.

Strangely enough, when I look back on my time on Skye, it's not the wildlife I remember most. It's one last evening in the Cuillin Hills Hotel. My clients then were in the main retired female schoolteachers. They were of course all dressed up in their finery after a good day on the hill and we enjoyed a good dinner together after which I challenged them to a game of rounders. There was a table tennis table with all the necessary equipment adjacent to the dining room and next door to the bar. They accepted the challenge and within moments had kicked off their shoes, and crying with laughter and shouting in excitement, these demure ladies raced around the table trying to get to one end in time to hit the ball back to the other. So much noise were they making, it brought everyone out from the bar to watch their antics but they didn't care a hoot. It's a memory I shall treasure till my dying day.

A comment by way of conclusion. In the '50s, it took me two days to reach Skye. Towards the year 2000 we would have breakfast at the Skye hotel on a Saturday, drive over the Skye bridge, take the southern route via Glen Sheil and Loch Ness to Inverness and arrive in time for everyone to catch the midday train to the south: a journey time of between two to three hours.

CHAPTER FOURTEEN

Boats and Boatmen: Island Travel in the 1960s

I HAVE MENTIONED some of the transport problems mountaineers had back in the 1950s; things improved, but were by no means 'plain sailing', as an account of some of the difficulties we faced on our safaris in the 1960s will show. By the very nature of the geography of Scotland's west coast, if you are going to spend some time there you will almost certainly spend some time in a boat. The boats and their owners can provide a wealth of experiences and stories and here I have put a few together to give a flavour of these. In the early days it was sometimes quite difficult to find someone who would take us to a particular island or the top end of a sea loch, but with some perseverance we usually came across a boat somewhere with an owner who was quite keen to get there himself and we provided the opportunity and monetary incentive to do so.

On occasion we tried to get to the Crowlin Islands just to the north of Kyle of Lochalsh and under the shadow of the Applecross hills where Gavin Maxwell spent a short time. At that time Applecross was fairly isolated. The only road in was the Bealach nam Ba (Pass of the Cattle) which climbs to a height of 2,006ft from Loch Kishorn. One consequence was that the school children of Applecross were ferried back and fore to Kyle of Lochalsh for some part of their schooling. We approached the owners of the ferry and they proved very willing to take our groups to the Crowlin Islands, dropping us off on their way to Toscaig to pick up the children in the morning and picking us up again in the afternoon. The ferry was named the Vital Spark and was obviously named after the boat featured in the Para Handy stories. It was quite a good boat and never let us down, though I can recall one occasion where there was only the one person in charge of the boat and he thought there was something not quite right about the way the engine was behaving. As we crossed the mouth of Loch Carron he disappeared into the bowels of the ferry and we heard loud hammer blows as he tried to either fix or release something. This went on for some considerable time and occasionally his head would appear through the hatch to make a 360 degree turn in order to see where exactly we were. We were quite relieved when he finally came topside as we approached the Crowlins.

This arrangement worked quite well until the road was built into the Applecross peninsula from the north and the school authorities changed the way the children were schooled and the ferry was no longer required. So we had to look around again for another means of access. Later in its life, the Vital Spark was moored at the pier in Kyle alongside a naval ship which was unloading dummy torpedoes for a testing range near Raasay. The onshore crane was not quite up to the load it was taking and toppled into the harbour taking the Vital Spark with it to the bottom. Evidently the hull was made of teak and the Vital Spark was refloated more or less intact.

Meanwhile we had spotted another possibility. There was a lovely looking boat which was berthed at Kyleakin across from Kyle. Eventually we traced the owner and discovered he was a Yorkshire man who hoped to run trips from Kyle. He was only too keen to take us to the Crowlins.

However, there was one snag here – he was much more interested in keeping his paintwork intact than making sure his passengers were happy. So he would take us within a yard of the small cliff that was the landing place and the passengers had to make the jump on to the island from there. We tried to persuade him that with an old tyre or fender, his paintwork would be quite safe but it fell on deaf ears.

This arrangement came to a very sudden end. He had made some friends in Kyle, though he lived across the water in Kyleakin. He was invited to a wedding and, naturally, rather than take the ferry, (this was long before the bridge was built) he would take his own boat across knowing that the regular ferry would have stopped for the night before the wedding ended. Unfortunately for him he had no idea of what a Highland wedding entailed and by the end of the night he could hardly stand. Nevertheless, he felt he could easily take the boat back to Kyleakin and at the highest state of tide he completely missed his usual berth and drove the boat high up the ramp used exclusively by the Skye ferry. Next morning, the tide had dropped leaving the boat high and dry and leaving the ferry nowhere to go. There were a few angry people around that morning and we never saw him again.

One of the most professional skippers we came across was Bruce Watt who owned a converted former wooden trawler named The Western Isles and did all the ferrying work in Loch Nevis. It was a trip everyone enjoyed, for we would set off from Mallaig and carry supplies to the Knoydart peninsula. This was some time before the area began to develop. We would then cross Loch Nevis to Tarbet where there lived the last remaining inhabitants of what had been a thriving fishing community when the movements of the herring shoals were reasonably predictable. When the railway finally reached Mallaig, rather than transport the herring by boat which was of course much slower, the railway took over the transport. Gradually the inhabitants of Loch Nevis gravitated towards Mallaig until only a few remained. Now, at Tarbet there were only an elderly brother and sister living here. The sister we never saw, for at the time she was quite frail and had a carer who would sometimes accompany us on the boat to look after her. Her brother however was very sprightly, though I think into his 80s.

Bruce couldn't get his boat close in to Tarbet, so always towed a small dinghy behind the larger vessel. This was brought alongside and all the provisions were loaded on board and a crewman would row it ashore where the old chap was waiting. The provisions usually included a 15kg bottle of calor gas and after the lighter provisions were unloaded the empty gas cylinder was put aboard the dinghy and the crewman rowed out to the Western Isles again. What happened next always filled me with admiration, for this old chap would simply hump the full cylinder on to his shoulder and, even at the lowest tide, boulder hop across the slippiest of rocks all the way to the shore and stride effortlessly to the house. I remember thinking at the time, 'If I can do that at his age, I shall be very, very happy.' Very often, we would disembark here by way of the dinghy, make our way through the narrow bealach behind Tarbet to Loch Morar and then down the lochside to the village of Morar some seven miles distant. Otherwise we would stay on the boat and Bruce would take us through the narrows into the upper reaches of Loch Nevis with its very spectacular peaks. On occasion Bruce would take us to Rum and it was on one of these trips that I discovered how good he was in handling his boat. The forecast was good and he had agreed to pick up two passengers at Ardvasar on Skye who were desperate to get on to Rum. As we left the shelter of Mallaig harbour, it was obvious a northerly gale was blowing straight down through the Inner Minch and we were taking it on the beam as we came into the quayside at Ardvasar. The waves were striking the quay and carrying spray up over the top keeping our two prospective passengers well back from the edge. With consummate skill, Bruce edged the vessel in carefully until the bow was riding up and down one of the heavy wooden fenders of the quayside. At the right moment he waved the two passengers aboard and they simply had to take one step from quayside to bow as easy as stepping off a pavement. He then reversed the vessel out of harm's way and we continued our journey.

As to Rum, I never felt comfortable on this island. There was something unwelcoming about it that reminded me strongly of the early days of belligerent landowners and disapproving Nature Conservancy. It's true that the conservancy used it as an experimental workshop for the management of deer but for some reason it had not lost its inability to welcome visitors even when the whole ethos of SNH changed for the better. I never experienced this on any other island, which were without fail very welcoming.

Because we used so many boats off the west coast for so many years, we came to know several of them very well, even with different owners. We had known the Shearwater since the very early days of going out to the Summer Isles off Ullapool so we were very pleased when we discovered that she was now owned by Murdo Grant at Arisaig. The Shearwater was a converted motor torpedo boat and Murdo used it to service the island of Eigg. At that time, there was a rock bar across the entrance to the mouth of the harbour of Eigg which meant that the ferry which serviced the Small Isles three times per week couldn't get in and everything had to be transferred from the larger vessel on to a small boat. The Shearwater ensured that the islanders had a means of getting off and on the island most days of the week and would take in smaller supplies for the inhabitants.

The crossing was always interesting, for in the early days of summer it was a good place for sightings of minke whales. Their whereabouts was made easier to detect, for where there were large numbers of gulls and seabirds feeding there would often be a minke whale and the Shearwater crew were very happy to divert the vessel to have a closer look. It was also a good place to see real shearwaters who nested in burrows on the hills of Rum. Eigg has had a chequered history of indifferent owners over many years – which has been well documented – but happily, with new legislation, the inhabitants were able to buy the island and now it appears to be a thriving community. We never had quite long enough on the island to get to the top of the Sgurr but there are many walks around it which were very productive from a naturalists point of view.

If I were forced to make a choice as to what makes the best boat journey off the west side of Scotland it would be very difficult, for they all have something unique. But if I were really pushed then I would have to choose the Treshnish Islands off Mull. Mull is a very rewarding island for anyone interested in natural history and we have spent many happy weeks over the years exploring all aspects of the island. But the highlight has always been a visit to the Treshnish Islands. Iain Morrison has been running Turus Mara

(Sea Tours) for as long as we have been visiting Mull and as was our usual custom, we would phone Iain the night before when we were sure a good day was forecast and we would set off from the harbour near Ulva.

Iain would take the boat out on to Loch na Keal and round the south edge of Ulva, past little Colonsay and on to the island of Staffa. It didn't happen very often but in a flat calm he would be able to take the boat right into Fingal's Cave and allow his passengers to disembark to explore this amazing place. Its columnar basalt structure has been described many times and every one of the superlatives is well deserved but it's only when you have experienced it that you feel its true splendour. The contraction of cooling lava had led to these wonderful geometric shapes. From the interior of the cave, it's possible to walk out and around to a point where a well-positioned ladder can get you up the cliff and on to the top where if you are fortunate you will discover a few puffins in the early summer months. Back on the boat, Iain heads westward. Due west we can see the Dutchman's Cap. Well named because of its shape, but we are heading north west toward Lunga on the Treshnish Islands. It's here we will see some of the most accessible seabird colonies of the west.

The landing at the north end of Lunga can be a little tricky, though by this time I am sure Iain will have found a good solution. Once ashore it's a very short walk to the grassy top where the puffins are nesting. Most people are very surprised that one, they are so tiny and two, they are so tolerant of all these camera-trigger happy people who can get within a metre or so of these colourful birds. Most people are trapped here, unable to tear themselves away from the puffins' antics but it's well worth walking to the south end of the island, to the Harp Rock. This is tightly packed with the relatives of the puffin, guillemots and razorbills with a number of shags dotted around, all intent on sitting tight on their egg. Patrolling the sky above are arctic and great skuas looking for any weakness or misjudgement of the birds below for they are always ready to pounce for the kill.

It's interesting how the tactics of the skuas vary from place to place. Usually they will harry one bird which they know is carrying food back to the nest. If it's a kittiwake, they will follow every twist and turn the unfortunate victim is forced to make until, exhausted, it disgorges the fish and the skua loses interest in the bird to pick up the disgorged fish. Sometimes they will simply dive on top of a guillemot or razorbill and force it down into the sea where once again the shocked bird disgorges.

Back on the boat, it's a case of rounding the island of Burgh to the north, then back into Loch Tuath to land at our starting point in late afternoon. It's here that I may have made a very bad faux pas for on one occasion many, many years ago, while coming in here, I saw a boat which was tied up in the shelter of a small island and putting my binoculars on it I could make out the name 'Vital Spark'. In my surprise I couldn't help shouting out in pleasure at seeing an old friend 'Oh, It's the Vital Spark.'

Iain said, 'Do you know it?'

'Yes' I said. 'Last time I saw it was on the bottom of the harbour at Kyle.'

'What!' shouted Iain. 'I've just bought it to restore.'

I could only say, 'Well it's a teak hull, so I'm sure it will be great when it's complete.'

From the Treshnish Islands one can see the Abbey on Iona and when on Mull it was always our habit to spend one day on the island. There is no doubt, there is a different atmosphere on Iona. It always seems tranquil. It was our habit to walk across to the west side of the island where there were usually a number of wading birds, then back to the abbey. Somewhere on the way, very often in the garden of the hotel, we would hear a corncrake. Its rasping call can be recognised by most people but it is seldom seen for it prefers to skulk in the undergrowth. My daughter Derry would often hear me talk of corncrakes and how they would make this rasping call. It was only when she went to stay with a school friend in Lewis that she discovered a corncrake had set up a territory under her bedroom window and craked all night that she heard it for the first time. It craked all and every night and when she came home, she said she didn't want to hear another corncrake as long as she lived. Iona is one of the few places in the Inner Hebrides where it still can be heard. Or at least it was back then.

When in the Abbey, I usually make straight for the cloisters for I have a keen interest in carving. The cloisters are supported by a series of slender twin columns and on the capitals are carved the most beautiful and delicate carvings of all the plants and birds one can find in the Highlands. The carvers really knew their birds and plants for they are instantly recognisable by their jizz, or how they behave in a certain way is always exactly right. For example, in their illustration of a diver on the nest turning eggs, it's obvious that the carver had actually witnessed this. The diver's legs are so far back on the body for swimming that it cannot walk on land and it always nests within a metre of the water. So it shuffles on to the nest and when turning the egg, it has to lift its entire body and move its head and neck in a beautiful arc to delicately move the egg to a new position under its body.

I would have loved to have known who the carvers were but couldn't find any reference to them at all. By a great coincidence, there lived in our village, Duncan Finlayson, a retired Church of Scotland minister in his 90s. I didn't get to know him till long after I retired but lo and behold, he was a young minister who had worked on the abbey in the 1960s and knew the carvers personally. He said there were two and they were entirely different from each other. One worked steadily every day while the other disappeared for days on end, then returned and worked furiously for another few days before disappearing once more. I like to think that the one who carved the birds spent a great deal of time observing the wildlife and returned to carve before the inspiration left him while the other methodically worked his way through the plants.

Before leaving the general area of Mull, Ardnamurchan and Sunart, it's worth noting that even in the time when otter numbers were considered to be very low many years back, this area could always be relied upon to produce a fair number of sightings of these attractive creatures, especially with a number of keen people armed with binoculars, continually scanning the coastline. It was often our practice that after a good day's walking and a very satisfying dinner, we would take the vehicle to a point on Loch Sunart where we could scan in both directions. With the vehicle acting as an excellent hide we were very often successful in spotting at least one otter and on the odd occasion a whole family. But perhaps the most surprising evening was one where we were sitting at this vantage point for some time and the light was beginning to fail. It was beginning to look like this might not be one of our lucky evenings when someone said they thought they had seen a movement on the shoreline some distance off. We all peered in the general direction and it certainly looked as if several creatures were moving towards us but they didn't have the gait of an otter. Then one turned slightly and we caught sight of a white patch on the chest. A family of pine martens.

The two youngsters were well ahead of the parents obviously enjoying what must have been an early taste of freedom for they were gambolling and inspecting any unusual object they spotted as they ran over the stony foreshore. We all tried to stay silent and as still as possible with binoculars glued to our face. As they came within a few yards, one of the parents suspected something and gave a single yelp. The youngsters immediately froze and didn't move a muscle until both parents were alongside. They had been well trained. One parent looked at the vehicle suspiciously. It was clear they came this way often and a new object near their path would have to be checked out. The parent was taking no chances and decided the safest thing to do was for the family to climb the bank, cross the single track road and disappear into the undergrowth on the other side.

We all relaxed, put our binoculars down with aching arms and were saying how marvellous an observation that had been, when someone on the other side of the vehicle said, 'There they are again,' and sure enough it seems they were determined not to be put off their usual trail and had simply given us a wide berth by making a wide arc behind us and resumed their journey along the shore. It was around this time that a local who rented out a holiday house had discovered that pine martens had taken up residence somewhere in the roof space in the house. They were undeterred by the house being occupied occasionally and in fact became quite used to being fed boiled eggs and jam in the late evening.

We usually visited Islay either very early or very late in the year when the geese were around and we combined this visit with one to Jura which has a totally different geology and is therefore a complete contrast to its neighbour. Though all the geese were mainly on Islay, it was our preference to stay on Jura which is much wilder. We would dearly have loved to find a boat and boatman to explore the west side of Jura, for it is difficult of access otherwise, but no one could ever be found, so we had to content ourselves by using the narrow single track road which runs up the east side of the island.

From this road one can access the Paps of Jura and the west side of the island near Tarbert, but our favourite walk was to the northern tip. The Jura Hotel at that time would very kindly lend us their largest Land Rover to make the journey, for the surfaced road peters out near Lealt after which it becomes an incredibly rough track which no ordinary vehicle should ever attempt. From this point we would bump along at no more than 5mph to Barnhill where George Orwell had lived. At the time the house was empty and we would have a look around the environs. It really is an incredibly remote place. Evidently he used a motor bike to get there before changing to a car. I have no idea how long a 1940s car would have survived on this track, but I am sure the suspension would have given up the ghost after a very short time. Then it was onward to Kinuachdrachd where the track ends at a keeper's house. From this point it is about three miles walk to our destination the Gulf of Corrievreckan and the well-known whirlpool. Sitting at Carraig Mor, we could watch the brooding water and as the tide changed we could witness the tidal races where, famously, George Orwell was caught out in a small boat, losing an oar and only just managing to get clear of it by sheer luck.

Back at Kinuachdrachd we would occasionally come across the keeper, a man at that time of vivid imagination and a good story-teller. One story still sticks in my mind. He was out on a stalk one day with a client when they came across a good stag. The only snag was that it was a difficult uphill shot. The man was a good marksman and shot the stag cleanly but the bullet continued upwards over the top of the hill and started its downward trajectory. By chance, it was a Wednesday, the only day of the week the ferry went to Colonsay. The falling bullet hit the funnel of the ferry and landed at the feet of a passenger who kept it as a souvenir. Hmm, I wonder.

It's a very short ferry crossing from Jura to Islay but the tidal races between the two islands ensures the ferry is forced into a wide arc as it fights the strong currents to reach Port Askaig. Islay, of course, is the place for birds, mainly for white fronted and barnacle geese in very great numbers. The farmers here must be very tolerant, for even though there is a compensation scheme, they must lose great quantities of crops to these grazing thousands. It's also a great place for duck of all species but the one bird most people want to see is the chough. The chough is a member of the crow family, and was at one time fairly common but is now quite rare and difficult to find. Islay is one of the few places left on the UK mainland where with a little searching they can still be found. It's a little bigger that a jackdaw but has red legs and a long curving red bill and its chief method of feeding is to turn over cow pats to eat the insects beneath.

We soon found a headland in which we could reliably find the chough every year as long as there were cattle around, and we would wander around the perimeter taking care not to disturb anything as we scanned between the cows with binoculars. On one particular occasion we had been successful in locating the choughs and were sitting on top of a high bank at the road end eating our lunch when we saw a pick-up truck drive slowly up the track. It pulled up below and the driver got out and headed towards us. My heart sank. I had seen this kind of approach so often in the early days and it was usually a prelude to a rant that we had no business being there. I racked my brains as to what we might have done wrong but could think of nothing we had not done on other visits without any problem.

As he got nearer, I realised he had a grin on his face so perhaps it wouldn't be that bad. He must have recognised me from other occasions for he made straight for me.

'Hi,' he said. 'Had a good day?'

'Oh yes,' I said. 'Hope it's all right to go around the edge looking for chough.'

He waved his arm. 'Och, that's no problem. You are the first people I've seen and I just had to tell someone, I took some stock to the sale today and I've just heard on the phone I got an absolutely great price. I've never got anywhere near that before and I'm over the moon.'

What a relief. It's very embarrassing if you are responsible for a group of people being there and are confronted by an angry landowner. This approach was quite different and one I had not encountered before. It was preferable; thankfully the irate landowner is a dying species.

CHAPTER FIFTEEN

The Outer Edge:
Hebridean Adventures

AS THE YEARS progressed and transport and accommodation facilities improved we were able to go to ever more distant areas with our groups, including the magical Outer Isles, Tir nan Og, the Gael's land of eternal youth. The Outer Islands are much larger than one supposes. It is possible now with better ferry connections to travel right through the islands in a reasonably short time. Back then when the ferry connections were a little more difficult, we would split our visits into ten days in Lewis and Harris and ten days in the Uists and Barra. This would give us plenty of time in some places but not nearly enough in others. On Lewis and Harris, we would usually stay at Baile na Cille, a manse imaginatively converted by Richard Gollan into a comfortable guest house on the edge of Uig sands with a wonderful backdrop of the West Lewis hills. From here it's possible to explore the more remote places on the island.

It was hereabouts where the famous Lewis chessmen were found, those tiny, 12th century walrus ivory carved Viking chess pieces which so capture the imagination. More recent research has found that the chess pieces were probably found not on the sands of Uig Bay but a little farther south at Mealista. Whatever the case, there is no doubt the Viking influence here is considerable and recent digs around Bhaltos have revealed a great deal about the Viking way of life and death. We would wander down the short road south of Uig and stop at Mangersta, a tiny beach which takes the full brunt of any westerly gale. To be here at the peak of a storm is an experience never to be forgotten, for the crashing roar of the sea can be deafening and the spume is thrown so high that one cannot approach the edge of the beach. The one sight which startled me most here are familiar green cushions of moss campion, for it is a plant I would expect to see on top of the Cairngorms. Just one indication of the extreme climate to be found here at sea level.

Just a little further on between the road and the cliff are the remains of a Norse 'click' mill, so called from the sound it makes. It was here centuries before the road was built and one can see the remnants of the lade leading into the mill itself, now in ruins but showing how the rushing water would turn the paddles of a horizontal wheel which in turn would spin the shaft leading up to the grinding stone. I have always felt it difficult to believe that a design so inefficient would be so widespread, for these mills can be found all over the islands, but then I am looking from a 21st-century perspective where technology has moved so fast it's difficult to keep up. It's probably the case that most small communities had these mills and their needs were so small that the output was very satisfactory. Once you get your eye in as to what to look for, like the small lintel which usually survives the collapse of the mill, you see them everywhere.

The surfaced road terminates at Breinis but a good track continues southwards, where early in the year we would see large flocks of golden plover before they split up and began nesting. Their plaintive call drew our attention for on the ground they are difficult to spot. A little further on at Mealista is where there used to be a rough sign which indicated that this was the site of a nunnery and there was indeed a cobbled floor but not much else. The most recent publication by the National Museums of Scotland claims this was most probably the place where the Lewis chessmen were actually found though the spelling, Mealasta, is slightly different. The track finally terminates at a small slipway and from here the going is largely trackless and tough going. But with a pair of binoculars looking south, one can see the island of Scarp, off the west side of Harris. It looks deceptively close and easy to reach on foot but don't be fooled, for any such undertaking involves mile upon mile of detours round various sea lochs.

To get to Harris from Uig involves a journey almost all the way back to Stornoway, then south down the east side of Lewis. The geology of Lewis is such that any road building is extremely difficult for the bed rock is Lewisian Gneiss one of the oldest and hardest on the planet. The same rock is found in the Shield area of Canada, and this fact helped to explain the drifting continent theory so one can sympathise with any road builder here. Harris is full of high hills with their heads in the clouds and with their feet on the beaches and the sea. Each of these has a unique character which makes it difficult to choose a favoured spot but certainly I would put Huis-inis, at the western extremity of North Harris near the top of my list. It has a beach facing north and just a few hundred yards away across a sandy track over the machair, another facing south. The island of Scarp is only a stone's throw away. It is well documented that a trial run of delivering post by rocket was attempted here in the 1930s, but unfortunately the rocket blew up on the way and the post was destroyed. A good idea but long before its time.

My best memory of this place is of being there on an idyllic day and walking on the little track from Huisnis to Crabhadail. The first part of the track climbs the hill and is directly above the sea. It was very still with the water green and flat. Gannets loved it here and we were at exactly the height where they were wheeling and diving just a few yards out from the cliff. From here one could follow their fishing technique. They would circle at our eye level and spot a fish below the surface. With a movement I can only describe as a cartwheeling motion, they would lower one wingtip and the other vertically then close the wings till the bird became the perfect arrow and sped downwards. The air was so still we could hear a little plop as they hit the surface then we could follow their movements underwater as they chased and caught the unwary fish to emerge on the surface again. Each and every dive perfect. Luskentyre on South Harris has the same kind of serenity but with the hills of North Harris as a backdrop. At the right tide, here was a good place for duck of varying species. I remember having excellent views of long tail ducks here effortlessly riding out quite stormy conditions and of eagles above Beinn Dubh.

St Clement's church at Rodel was the southernmost point of our visits to Lewis and Harris and we could look across the Sound of Harris to the lower hills of North Uist not all that far away but in those days, to get on to the Uists from South Harris meant retracing ones steps to Tarbert, then taking the large ferry to Lochmaddy. This ferry had then a triangular run from Uig on Skye to Tarbert on Harris, then it went Harris to Lochmaddy then back to Uig and its timings were tricky for us in various ways, so when a direct ferry was introduced from Leverburgh on South Harris to Bernaray and North Uist, we were first in the queue.

I love every ferry crossing in the west of Scotland but this was always one of my favourites, especially on a good day in early spring. The Sound is full of skerries and shallows which means the ferry has to twist and turn quite a lot. Birds seem to love it at this time of year for the Sound must provide good feeding and shelter from the elements and one can see large numbers of eider duck, the males in really good black and white plumage, great northern divers heading north to their breeding grounds in the Arctic in all states of plumage from their dowdy winter state to full blown breeding plumage of black head with a narrow white ring round the neck and a beautiful chequered black and white pattern on their back. Lots of red breasted mergansers are to be seen, and of course the usual seabirds, with shags drying their wings on the skerries and auks racing back and forth in every direction. In short, a crossing full of interest while the views of Harris looking back are wonderful. The whole scene a kaleidescope of colour from the emerald green of the shallows through to the deep blue of the deeper water, the yellow of the lichens on the skerries and foreshores and the hazy purple hills of Harris.

Balranald on North Uist became famous in the bird world many years ago when a pair of snowy owls nested there, and in consequence, the area was taken over as a reserve. As far as I know, the snowy owl, a bird of the Arctic, no longer visits, but it's an interesting place nevertheless. We would often have a walk around its perimeter, for depending on the time of year it produced some interesting birds. On the shoreline feeding among the kelp, one would often find large flocks of sanderling and dunlin while inland one is bombarded by the sound of the corncrake but most interesting of all is another sound largely unheard now in most parts of the country. It's the voice of the corn bunting which is usually described as the sound of jangling keys. They are a somewhat nondescript small bird which sits on a prominent place and with open mouth emits this curious sound. They were widespread throughout the British Isles at one time but changing farming methods meant a collapse in their numbers and rather like the corncrake can only be found in areas where traditional farming methods are still prevalent.

One can walk for miles on the machair and beaches on the west side of South Uist stopping on occasion to look at the myriads of small flowers on this carpet of colour immediately inland of the sea. Shell sand blown up from the shoreline ensures this remains a fertile but delicate strip of land. The crofters will cultivate a small patch and move to another area to let it recover the next year. This rotation ensures the machair will survive.

Rubha Airdbhule just west of Bornish, about halfway down the west side of South Uist, is one of the most wonderful places both scenically and for the keen bird watcher. This tight little area produces all kinds of interesting things for it contains a small lochan good for nesting – but more than that, it is an incredible viewpoint of the whole island for one has stepped back as it were. To the north and south, as far as the eye can see, stretches the continuous beach vibrant in the sun, while inland are the blue hills of Beinn Mhor, Ben Corodale and Hecla filling the horizon to the east.

It was our habit in those early days to spend most of our time on South Uist and from this base to have a day on Eriskay and another on Barra. This was mainly because the vehicle ferry connection from South Uist to Barra would only go on certain days and even then it would be a late evening journey. There was, however, a foot passenger ferry operated by Donald Campbell which ran from Ludaig on South Uist to Eoligarry on Barra and a small vehicle ferry which connected Eriskay to Uist. Eriskay is a lovely little island which is easy to explore entirely on foot. So we would leave our vehicle behind and take the ferry across to Haun and walk round to the beaches on the west side. It's here that Bonnie Prince Charlie first set foot on Scottish soil and is still called the Prince's Strand.

For a number of years, I had an excellent guide, for there was a collie which had a look out point above the beach and when the dog spotted us he would dash down and greet us like old friends. He would know our routine and walk just a few steps ahead of us the whole day. A very polite dog that, when we settled down to have lunch, would sit a few yards away with his back to us and would only approach us if he was called in for a titbit, returning to his station to eat it. One thing which intrigued me on Eriskay back then was that someone was still using the age old system of cultivation known as lazybeds. The regular visitor to the Highlands and Islands will have noticed, when the light is at the right angle, a series of small furrows and ridges on every hillside capable of growing anything. This is where the local inhabitants have opened up the soil, spread seaweed as a compost, planted potatoes and piled the soil in ridges for drainage to produce a good crop. Here we could actually still see how it was done. The person still using this method always kept the plot in immaculate condition and gave the lie to the name lazybeds for it looked like very hard work.

At the end of the beach we would climb a short distance, passing through great clumps of iris to join the single track road which crosses the island to Acarsaid Mor (the great anchorage) where there is another small community. For several years in succession the only post box here had a sign saying. 'Please do not post letters in this box, we have a robin nesting inside. Leave letters in the box provided below.' We would occasionally see a golden eagle around this area. We guessed it nested on the eastern flank of the island, which is largely uninhabited and, having scanned the area, we would begin the walk back to the ferry. At a certain point, the collie would come up to us, wag its tail as a goodbye and disappear over the horizon.

On one occasion we had not seen the eagle and had returned to the ferry where we were waiting for the boat to cast off. I was still hoping for a glimpse of the raptor and I was scanning with binoculars along the top edge of Ben Scrien, the only reasonably high eminence on the island, when I came across a sheep grazing steadily along the very edge of the hill. Just as I was passing over it with my binoculars, the animal slipped and started tumbling down the hillside. I am used to sheep being very sure footed and if they make a wrong move they recover quickly. This one didn't. It left the ground and was spinning, then hit the ground several times more as it descended head over heels until it finally stopped on a flat area just above Haun. I reckoned it must be dead, but no, it immediately stood up and started grazing again as though nothing had happened. No one else appeared to have witnessed this so I asked the crewman if he knew who owned the sheep on the hill. He did, of course, and I told him what happened and he assured me he would tell the owner to have a look. I hope he did.

On another day, again on foot, Donald would take us across to Eoligarry in his small boat and leave us on this northern end of Barra. It was on one of those days that I decided that I had to spend much more time on the island. In fact, even now – long, long after retirement, if someone asks, 'What is your best island day, ever?' This was it. When I was a boy in Aberdeen in war time, like many others of my age, our chief source of entertainment was the cinema. At the time most American films were in Technicolour. How I wished real life were in those vivid colours. Well on Barra on this day it was. But that was only one part of the whole scene. Words are never enough to describe something that is a total experience when everything comes together at one and the same time.

It was a day of total clarity where one could pick out detail miles away. The sea is very shallow coming in to the jetty at Eoligarry so the water is a vivid emerald because of the sandy bed. As soon as the engine cut out, the air was filled by the singing of countless numbers of skylarks. As we walked from Eoligarry toward the churchyard where Compton MacKenzie is buried, the skylarks were joined by the piping of redshanks which were nesting in the fields on either side. Intent on distracting us from their nests they were flying ahead of us and alighting on the fence posts allowing us close enough to see (without binoculars) their bright red legs and bill. The fields themselves were filled with the lush green vegetation and yellow flowers of marsh marigolds interspersed with primrose as far as the eye could see. Within this dense cover there lurked numerous corncrakes, their rasping love-call contrasting with the melodious sound of the songbirds.

It was an easy walk. We were making for Dun Scurribhal, the remains of an iron age fort on a small hill which commands views in every direction. The builders chose the position well, for on this day one could see the entire length of the Uists to the north. To the west lay the great sweep of the Atlantic, while to the south and east one looks over a narrow neck of the island and the beaches of Traigh Eais and Traigh Mor where the airfield lies. The only airport on the British Isles to be swept by the sea every day. From the Dun it is a very easy climb on short turf to the summit of Ben Eoligarry. On this day the hill was a carpet of interesting flowers, heath spotted, early purple and small white orchids along with the occasional fragrant orchid. All very tiny, a reflection of the harsh winter conditions in these parts but this was no problem for the primroses, for they again were everywhere. A stretch out in the sun on the summit and on a day when nothing could go wrong, the tides were just right for us to watch the daily flight from Glasgow circle above us then make a short descent to alight on the Traigh Mor and see the passengers disembark and walk across the sand to the airport building. Then it's a leisurely walk down the hill and along the road back to Eoligarry in time for Donald to pick us up and return us to the Uists. The perfect day.

The following year, I decided to change the arrangements for the Uists and split our time between Uist and Barra. This meant we spent the first few days on Uist, then round about 9.00pm in the evening we would join the car ferry which left Lochboisdale and carry us down to Castlebay on Barra. This was a very enjoyable trip, where the ferry carried us well out into the Minch then southwards to Barra. Many times we were fortunate enough for it to be an impressive sunset where the various islands would be silhouetted against an orange sky. Arriving in Castlebay around midnight, we would drive the short distance to the hotel and, as best we could, find our rooms without disturbing the other guests.

I always took the precaution of phoning John Alan McNeil on Barra the night before we left Uist, for we always hoped to get to Mingulay and he was the perfect man to take us there. We had three full days on Barra and wanted to have the best of the three reserved for a possible visit. I arranged with John that he was to phone me at the hotel as soon as he heard a good forecast. I could then prepare everyone for the journey. As soon as I was called to the phone, I knew the trip was on. So at 9.30 the next morning we were boarding John's boat and heading south. In the main we were very fortunate in our weather and we were soon heading out past Kishmul castle and on our way down the east side of Bhatersay. Behind, bobbing and darting in our wake, we towed a dinghy. When we arrived at Mingulay it would be necessary for us to transfer into the smaller boat to be ferried ashore in small groups of four for though there was an enticing beach on which to land, it was well known as a place to avoid because of the undertow. In the meantime, we had a long pleasant journey ahead of us with plenty of time to enjoy the sun, seabirds and spectacular outlines of Rum and Skye to the north and east.

John Alan is a shy, modest man but once the formalities are over, one discovers he has a great sense of humour and a remarkable knowledge of the area both past and present. His mother was born on Mingulay. In fact, when Robert M Adam, the famous Scottish photographer, visited Mingulay in 1905, among the many excellent photographs taken is one of John's mother as a girl in her early teens with her younger sister and brother. Alas, when Adam took those historical photographs, the island was already in steep decline. It was always a precarious place to live and by 1912 it was empty. Mingulay's massive west-facing cliffs, thronged with seabirds in the spring and early summer, take the full brunt of the Atlantic gales and the island's inhabitants wrested a precarious living from the relatively sheltered east-facing slope leading down to a sandy bay. Like the St Kildans, they reaped a harvest from the seabirds by clambering about these awesome cliffs and we heard tales of how they would row a boat into the narrow gap between the main cliff and the rock stack of Lianamul, jump on to the guano encrusted ledge, climb the Stack harvesting birds as they went and dropping the carcasses down on to the bobbing boat below. Though on occasion we had been able to get round the west side of the island by boat in previous years, the violent back wash off the base of the mighty cliff had prevented us from glimpsing this tiny gap. But we lived in hope.

In the years following Adam's visit, living on the island became ever more precarious. In order to support their families, a few menfolk had gone to the mainland for work, sending back whatever they could. This in turn meant a reduction in manpower required for launching boats and harvesting both crops and birds. By 1912, those remaining, John Alan's grandfather among them, decided living there was no longer viable and applied to the then landowner for some ground on Bhatersay. When refused, they took the law into their own hands and made a land raid on Bhatersay setting up huts and small-holdings. Despite legal attempts to evict them, they would not be moved. But that is a whole story in itself, very well told by Ben Buxton in his book *Mingulay*. Suffice to say that John Alan's mother, Catherine, who was probably around the age of 17 at this time, decided to move to Edinburgh where she worked as a tram conductress before returning to Barra. A remarkable move for a young girl who had probably never been off Mingulay.

Our journey took us down the east side of Sandry and Pabbay, making the most of any shelter offered by these islands – although today was looking good and the sea fairly flat. Between these last two islands John pointed out the small island of Lingay. A tiny island with no obvious landing place.

Evidently, peat was becoming quite scarce on Mingulay and the story is that the men of Mingulay would often take peat from Lingay. To get the fuel off the island when it was dry, they would line the bottom of a boat with turf, lead two ponies on to the boat and row it across to Lingay, and use the ponies to carry the peat down to the boat and then row the whole lot back to Mingulay.

There it was, dead ahead, the awesome 750ft vertical cliff of Buillacraig on Mingulay, shimmering in the heat of a flat calm sea. With conditions this good, we should surely get down the west side? Non-committal as ever, John said, 'We'll have a look at it,' and we kept heading for the cliffs. These were easily the best conditions we had seen, hardly a ripple and the sun reflecting strongly off the surface. Already we could hear the echoing calls of the kittiwakes, the gargling of the auks and the cackle of the fulmar. Then we were right under the cliffs surrounded by wheeling, diving, screeching birds, each one intent on its own particular business.

'Where exactly can you see the gap between the cliff and the Stack of Lianamul?' we asked.

Cagey as ever, John replied, 'We'll have a look.'

He walked back to the stern and pulled our obedient dinghy close behind the boat and secured it hard against the stern before heading directly for the cliff face which twisted and turned so much we couldn't distinguish between cliff and stack. But John knew exactly where he was going. Just when we appeared to be heading straight for the cliff with no way out, a swift turn and there we were in an incredibly narrow passage. There was only just enough room for the boat to scrape through. Cliffs rose vertiginously on either side and we marvelled at the confidence of the islanders in jumping off the boat on to slippery rocks, climbing upwards, gathering birds and throwing them down to the waiting boat. On the way down past Pabbay we had spotted a few young climbers who were looking for new rock climbing routes on the cliffs there. They were well equipped with all the climbing gear necessary these days. They would have been well in tune with the islanders of Mingulay for they too revelled in their climbing abilities. The difference being that while present day youngsters did it for fun, back then it was purely for food. Plus the fact the islanders had only the most basic of equipment, a rope and probably bare feet.

We moved slowly between these towering cliffs, totally hemmed in it seemed, but John was looking ahead and astern all the time. He was looking for some markers which were visible only to him and we made a sudden turn to the right and there ahead lay the open sea again. There was only just enough room for the boat and dinghy to make the turn in one manoeuvre and now we understood why the dinghy was brought right up to the stern earlier. The engine was opened up and we pulled away from the cliff, and we sped round the south end of the island and through the gap which separates Mingulay from Berneray (Barra Head) the final island in the chain. Soon we were drifting quietly in the clear water of Mingulay bay, our landing place.

The beach looks a very tempting place to land but as explained earlier, it had its problems with undercurrents, so John would land us on a small cliff slightly north of the ruined village. He usually had a young lad with him and while John looked after the boat, the young lad would row us ashore in groups of four. It was my usual habit to go on the first group so that I may assist them ashore and up the cliff before returning to fetch the next group. On one early visit, I had a slightly disabled person with me and thought it better to stick close by to be of more assistance. One of our group had been with me on Mingulay before. Molly was probably our best botanist and I asked her if she remembered the route up the cliff. She said she did, so I asked her if she would go in the first group while I stayed with the boat and helped the disabled person. She readily agreed as it would give her slightly more time to botanize.

Once again I was organising the next group when I glanced ashore to see how the others were faring. To my horror, Molly had taken the wrong route and was heading for a difficult section of rock. I shouted a warning not to go any further and wait till we got ashore. When we were all gathered at the foot of the cliff, I asked Molly if she could get back down to us. The reply was an emphatic, 'I'm certainly NOT coming back down.' So having made sure the others were on the right route, I returned to Molly who at that time was probably in her sixties and well built. She said it would be easier for her to continue upwards for she would find it much more difficult to come down. So we worked out a route which would take her along a ledge with good handholds and then on to the usual route. With me climbing along below her, it somehow gave her enough confidence to do the traverse even though we both realised if she came down on top of me there was no way I could stop us both from going down together. Much to everyone's relief, we reached the cliff top without mishap. That part of the cliff was always known afterward as Molly's Crag.

The cliff top here also happens to be a puffin colony, so it's a case of getting everyone across and on to the flatter part of the island as soon as possible. The first thing which strikes you, or rather it did then, was the appearance of a fairly large double storeyed building totally enveloped by a striking yellowish orange lichen. This was the church. It had the priest's quarters on the lower storey and an outside stairway leading up into the church itself.

On our earliest visits, this building was more or less complete but gradually it deteriorated over the years and at one point a gap appeared between the roof and west wall where the wind had found a way in. Then when we returned on a visit in 1996, the roof, made entirely of heavy slate, had been lifted clean off the building and deposited in front – more or less in one piece. A wind capable of doing this is very hard to imagine. The rest of the village is in ruins and is being claimed by the sand as is the burial ground but it is still possible to make out John's mother's house for there is a particularly large stone to the left of the doorway in the 1905 photograph that is still intact today. The only building still being maintained on our last visit is the old schoolhouse which lies further round the bay from the main village and is used by shepherds and visitors.

Above the village, the fields, where so much back-breaking work had gone in to make them fertile, remained much as they were left. One can still easily discern the well-made roadway leading from the village to the school. What makes the whole scene more poignant is that because of Adam's visit in 1905, we can put faces and names to all those who once lived there. Was he the unwitting recorder of a community in its death throes or did he go there in the knowledge that it couldn't last much longer? My last visit there was in 2000 when the future of the islands was once more in the balance. Since 1955 they had been owned by the Barra Head Isles Sheepstock Company but the steep falls in sheep prices made it no longer viable to keep sheep there. The sheep were gathered and taken off and the islands of Mingulay, Pabbay and Berneray put up for sale. I see now the islands are owned by the National Trust for Scotland which I suppose was inevitable. I do hope they will remain difficult to access for large bodies of people; though they have their place, large groups of people have a habit of taking the adventure out of everything and making things somewhat bland. Long may the archipelago remain difficult of access.

CHAPTER SIXTEEN

Flying High, Flying Free: Eagles

IF ASKED WHAT was my favourite bird, I might possibly reply that it is the golden eagle. On occasion, watching them soar made me feel somewhat akin to them; I had escaped from a life of industrial servitude and had been fortunate enough to also soar in my element, the great outdoors. My first encounter with eagles was in my teens. There were three of us walking in single file on a narrow track below Beinn a' Bhuird in the eastern Cairngorms. We were intent on reaching Corrie an Dubh Lochan where we hoped to complete a rock climb and were moving quite quickly, for this would have been round about 1951 and we had no transport which meant we had to do the climb, return to our tent five miles behind us, then walk another six miles down the glen in time to catch a bus which left Braemar at 7.00 in the evening. Our concentration was entirely on what lay ahead.

To our great surprise, a red grouse dropped from the sky immediately over our heads and scuttled under a boulder. We were used to grouse rising in front of us but to have one drop and hide by our feet was almost was unheard of. We looked upwards as a shadow passed over us and we located this massive bird already in an upward swoop having just missed its prey most probably because of our presence. The eagle hung above our heads for a few moments then sheered away to pass out of sight over a ridge. On reflection, I can remember every second of that encounter but nothing at all about the climb we were intent on completing. The second encounter was probably with the same bird or its partner on the same hill the next year. It was late spring and we were trying to extract the maximum use of the remaining snow by carrying skis into a shallow corrie which hung on to the last of the snow. It was a warmish day and we stopped about halfway up to the snowline and all stretched out in the sunshine. I had my eyes closed and someone said quietly, 'Look at that.' I opened my eyes and there directly above us an eagle hung motionless over our heads.

We lay still while the eagle scrutinized us. 'Does it think we might be carrion?' someone asked.

'Well, I'm not waiting to find out,' someone else said and we all picked up our skis quickly and resumed our climb.

It may have been late the same year that we were walking out through the tree line of the Ballochbuie Forest when Charlie, the eldest of our group and the most experienced, drew our attention to a dead scots pine, saying. 'There's been an eyrie on that tree for years and years.' It must be remembered that there were no rules regarding wildlife in those days so we felt no compunction about going to have a closer look. It was evident that the tree had been dead for a number of years; whether killed by a lightning strike or the activities of the eagle no one could be sure. There now remained a smooth trunk perhaps 20ft high, with a great fork beyond in which the eyrie sat. It looked very deep and had obviously been added to over many years.

'I think I'd like to have a look inside,' Charlie said. And we contemplated how it may be done, considering it as a climbing challenge. We all carried rope slings around our waist then for we were still keen rock climbers. 'I think with a sling around the tree and leaning out far enough to brace against the trunk, I could get up there,' Charlie continued. He was the shortest of our group and we thought he might have the best chance. At that time, we were still climbing in heavily serrated nailed boots called tricounis and the nails would get a good purchase against the trunk. So off he set while we watched. It required a few failed attempts but eventually he mastered the technique and reached the fork on which the eyrie rested. What struck us immediately was just how tall the nest was for with Charlie standing alongside, he could only just peep over the top into the cup.

'There's lots of stuff in here,' he shouted down and reaching into the cup threw down various bones of numerous prey. We picked them up as they fell, trying to identify what they could be.

There were all kinds of rib baskets, maybe mountain hares? And bird skulls. Grouse? We pondered over these and concluded the eyrie was no longer in use as there was no recent sign of occupation, as the remains he found had all been there for some considerable time. After this the golden eagle simply became part of the landscape just like the deer, grouse ptarmigan and hare. It was of passing interest. The main focus was still on rock.

More than a decade on, wildlife had become our way of life and the golden eagle was of renewed interest. I made an application to the Nature Conservancy for a permit to look at eagles' eyries in Ross and Sutherland and was allowed to do this for two or three years. It was fascinating. Because the eagle takes such a long time to incubate the eggs and for the young to leave the nest, it has to start very early in the year. So late in January would see Derek and I wandering up various glens looking for displaying birds. It would perhaps be of interest here to describe one of the best displays we had ever come across. It was a crisp morning in late January. There was a clarity in the atmosphere which you only get at this time of the year: a deep frost at dawn leading to a clear blue sky with deep snow in the glen. We spotted the eagle high above a rocky peak and thinking we might see a hunt or be lucky enough to observe a display we lay down on the snow with binoculars in gloved hands and elbows resting on our chest, the best position for lengthy high viewing of this nature.

The bird seemed to be soaring much higher than usual, using any uplift from the steep rocky cliff below, though this would be minimal in the prevailing conditions. So high did it soar that we lost sight of it with the naked eye and we had great difficulty in picking it up again against the clear blue sky with no cloud shapes for rough guidance of the binoculars. But we were still both onto it when the eagle suddenly closed its wings completely and plummeted toward the hill. We expected it to flatten out, but it didn't – it just kept plummeting earthwards faster and faster until as the bird and the rocky peak came into the same binocular view, we were shouting at each other. Then just as we thought we were witnessing the first eagle suicide, the wings shot out and were thrust into a violent upward curve by the sheer air pressure on the underwing and the bird beautifully converted its downward plummet into a graceful upward soar. The eagle repeated this maneouvre several times over the course of the next hour or so. Each time it was as thrilling as the last and we guessed that the female was sitting on the crag somewhere full of admiration – as we certainly were. We scanned the cliff but couldn't pick her out. The other piece of display which we hoped to see was when the pair meet high in the air, locked talons and spiralled downwards only to separate at the last moment. I have only seen this once or twice but did not on this occasion.

Each eagle pair may have several nesting sites on their territory and the trick is to discover which one they might use that year. They will repair and add new material to the chosen nest and the first egg of perhaps two is usually laid about the third week in March. Incubation takes around 40 days and the chicks hatch out around the first week in May. The chicks are delicately fed by the parents for the first two or three weeks, the adult tearing into the prey and feeding each chick with the softer parts. Later the chicks have no apparent problem tearing into the prey themselves and by the ninth week it is difficult for the parent even to land for the chicks are craning at the edge of the nest eager to be the first to secure whatever may be brought in.

One of the memories which has stayed with me over the years has been sitting on the opposite side of the glen at about the same level as one eyrie and having an excellent view with binoculars and telescope of the activity at this time. The skyline above the nest was more or less horizontal and I could usually see the parent return from a long way off.

On this occasion, I couldn't believe my eyes. I could see this massive thing floating just out from the edge of the cliff. This can't be a bird, can it? It looked at this distance like a small helicopter. But no. When I put the binoculars on it, it was one of the parents with a gigantic haunch of a deer held in its talons. It was at its

maximum carrying capacity and obviously had the greatest difficulty in staying in the air. It hung out a few yards from the edge of
the cliff and made use of the updraught to struggle about one mile
distant toward the nest. There was never a wing beat, it just
allowed the air current to carry it forward. The two chicks, of
course, had noticed long before I did and they were each on the
edge of the nest straining forward. They were around nine weeks
old by this time and within a week or so would be leaving the nest.
Their combined bulk filled the edge of the nest and I could see no
way that the parent could possibly alight. But it had no intention
of doing so. When it was almost level with the nest, the parent
swung out then revolved its whole body and literally threw the
gigantic piece of prey in between the chicks onto the floor of the
nest. A neat piece of aerobatic skill. The two chicks were on to the
meat immediately and were already devouring it as the parent flew
off again. It was clear the adults has found a deer carcase and
were, over a lengthy period, dissecting it and carrying the dismem-
bered pieces back to the eyrie.

Both chicks had been vigorously exercising their wings over the
previous few weeks and next time I returned one chick had already
left the nest. The other was still on the edge, still undecided. One
parent was yelping at the other side of the glen and at last the
remaining chick taking its life in its talons launched off the edge.
It had no knowledge of winds or updraughts so it wobbled quite
a bit, then a sideways wind caught it and the chick twisted and
turned to regain its equilibrium. By this time, it was more than two
thirds of the way across the width of the glen and it could see the
opposite hillside looming up directly in its path. There was only
one thing for it and that was to make a crash landing. It pitched
into the heather and tumbled some distance before coming to rest
and standing upright to retain its dignity. It yelped pitifully but the
parent continued to circle over head, for it knew hunger would
force the young bird off the ground again and within a few days
its flying skills would be as good as the parents.

I think it must have been in the very early '80s that I was

contacted by the RSPB who were thinking of making a film on the golden eagle and asked me if I would like to be involved as I had already been looking at several eyries over the preceding years. I was of course happy to do this but Highland Safaris would be taking up a large proportion of my time so I asked a good friend, Les Lamb, if he would be involved and step in to my place when I had to be away. Les was an excellent artist but didn't have to be at his easel at specific times so it was an arrangement that would suit everyone. Alan MacGregor would be doing all the camera-work and Alan duly arrived in the autumn prior to doing any filming so that we could both get acquainted and carry out lots of preparatory work for the next year.

The first task was to visit every nesting site I could think of so that we could discuss the degree of difficulty in getting in and out easily, setting up hides, carrying in equipment – and accessibility from the nearest road. We had to think of what plan would cause the least disturbance to the birds and not be noticed by the general public for it was vital to be as low key as possible. One of the greatest problems was that normally a pair of eagles would have anything up to three or four nesting sites to choose from on their territory. What makes them choose one site as opposed to another no one knows, but I would guess prevailing weather conditions at the time of repairing the nest and egg laying would figure largely in their choice. It has to be remembered that the first egg is laid usually in late March and winter snow can still lie deep near their nest while winds can be gale force quite regularly at that time of year.

Alan was keen to have as many fall back positions as possible so we chose three territories where we thought we would have the greatest chance of success. There was one territory where the eagles had used the same nest in the previous three years so we chose this as our primary objective.

The site was not particularly easy to get to, for it was on a ledge in the middle of a rock face. Using ropes, we looked at the nest from various angles around it to get the best camera angles and decided that if we built a supporting structure during the winter, slightly higher than the nest, so that the camera had an uninterrupted view into the cup, we could build a hide on top of this and have it in position before any courting began. Access from this position would be slightly easier without the use of ropes for it was important we could get the cameraman in and out in the shortest time, causing as little disturbance to the nesting pair as possible.

The other two nests were in separate glens further away and, having examined the area around each of the several nesting sites, we concluded that it would be possible to set up a hide nearby on most of those without any kind of underbuilding so we could leave this task till nearer the time. Alan spent the next two or three weeks wrestling with a Dexion angle iron to build a platform which could be fixed to the face of rock and by early winter this had been secured. Back at his base he spent some time constructing a fairly lightweight hide to bolt on to the platform. We would have to find a way to get this up the mountainside and this was never going to be easy.

Once the hide was complete we tested its weight and it was clear we were never going to get this up the hill without a desperate struggle. He had no alternative but to build it from a fairly solid material for the site was fairly exposed and we didn't want to have anything flapping around in the winds that would be certain to come along. There was only one thing for it – we would have to fly it in by helicopter. After some negotiation with the helicopter company, it was agreed if we could transport the hide on a trailer to the roadside nearest the nest, the pilot would pick it up, fly it up the hill and even lower it on to the platform. We would of course have to wait for a slot of good, still weather. This, we thought, was going to be the easiest part of our work. How little we knew.

Winter was with us now in good measure. There were several episodes of wind and snow and we could imagine what the conditions were like higher up the hill. But at last the day dawned. A phone call from the helicopter company. It would be clear and still round about the middle of the day and the helicopter would meet with us at the pre-arranged spot on the roadside. We sped up the road with the hide on the trailer and sure enough by midday the sky was clear and windless conditions prevailed. The helicopter alighted close by and the pilot shut down the engine and came across to see what the plan of action was to be. He inspected the hide and thought that, since there was so little weight, it would cause no problems, and we devised a method where we could suspend the hide below the helicopter. With a length of wire rope, we attached the centre point of the hide and hooked it under the helicopter. We then all climbed aboard and set off. This was going to be easy.

Guided by our instructions, the pilot flew us toward our objective, hide swinging slowly below us and as we got closer we could see the snow had been drifting quite a bit around the area of the nest site while the ridge by which we normally approached on foot was solid snow. We pointed out the platform of the rocky face and the pilot edged the helicopter as close as he dared but he looked very concerned. 'Sorry lads, this is going to be more difficult than I thought. We are so close to the rockface above the platform, I worry that any eddy of the wind may take me into the face – then we'll be in trouble. I don't think we can do it. Let's think of something else.' And so saying, he moved the machine away from the face and we hovered over the glen.

'I think the best and safest idea is for me to drop the hide and yourselves off on your approach ridge, then at least you will be able to carry it round to the platform between you. There will be no climbing to do. I will land you at a point on the same level as the platform.' It was the only sensible thing to do. By good luck, at the last moment I had taken my ice-axe with me, thinking I might need it at some point. So we flew in towards the hill again and the pilot gently lowered the hide on to the snow of the ridge beneath and alighted a few yards away, where we detached the wire rope. With a wave, the helicopter had gone.

It was immediately apparent that the snow was quite hard, and we had to cross a very steeply angled slope to get to the platform some three or four hundred yards away. If one of us slipped, the other, left with the full weight of the hide, would also fall and we had visions of the hide careering down the hillside on the hard snow. There was nothing else for it, we had to cut steps all the way round so that our boots could get a reasonable grip on the surface. This took a considerable time and it was late afternoon before we finally had the hide on top of the platform. It was then a case of bolting the hide to the platform. No easy task, for one of us had to take gloves off and fumble with frozen fingers to find the boltholes and push the bolts through while the other screwed them tight. It was almost dark by the time we got back to the vehicle and trailer.

It was now a case of waiting. Alan went south again to attend to some other filming business while I would on occasion have a look at our newly placed hide and check that all was well at the other territories. I would only see the eagles sporadically, for the area they covered was very wide and at this point of the year there was nothing to take them back to the nesting sites, for their biggest problem was finding enough prey to sustain the through the winter. March came in with its usual gales and late snow and I stepped up the visits to our chosen sites. There were some signs of courting and Alan came back up once more. Any film of court-ing display was almost impossible for it was difficult to anticipate when it might happen, and in any case the displays took place at too great a distance for it to be captured well on film.

Then on one visit to our prime pair, my heart sank. They were building, but not on the nest they had used for the last few years, but on another site farther across the same face but in a position where our substantial hide would be of no use whatsoever. We had to do a quick rethink. From below at a safe distance, where the activity was taking place, through binoculars, we could see a tiny heathery ledge on which perhaps a hide could only just about sit. We would leave them alone for the present and see what would develop. In the meantime, the other two pairs in which we were interested were showing signs that they were going to settle down on their usual ledge. We discussed our strategy. The prime pair were still our best bet. We thought that the potential for a hide to be positioned on the heathery ledge may well be a good one and decided that we should erect a hide on low ground which we could modify and make fairly rigid so that it didn't flap, even in a strong wind and that it could be well anchored so that it couldn't be moved off the spot in a gale. Finally, we practised putting it up and down for if we were to go up to the eyrie, we had to be in and out in a very short time to ensure that the eggs did not get cold.

At last, a warmish day and the birds were quite certainly sitting. We didn't want to startle the sitting bird so we climbed quite openly, sure in the knowledge that we were observed on our way up the hillside. We knew that at a certain point in our approach the eagle would come off the nest. Sure enough when we were still some distance off, the bird slipped off the nest and, keeping close to the hillside, slid round the edge of the ridge without a single wing beat. We immediately quickened our pace and within moments were on the heathery ledge, feverishly erecting the hide and securing it in position. Then we were off again and walking quickly downhill, panting heavily with the exertion and tension.

Would she accept it? We had taken a great deal of trouble to match contours and colouring to cause the least distraction but we could never be sure what might happen. In a few minutes we were on the floor of the glen where we lay down and watched anxiously through binoculars. It was a warm day and the eggs would be alright if they were uncovered for a short time, but we were prepared to dash up the hillside again if the eagle didn't put in an appearance in a very short time and take down the hide immediately. With great relief, we saw the bird slide round the ridge once more and settle back on the nest. Success.

We knew that the eggs had been laid probably no more than a week or so. They sit for around 40 days before hatching so we waited a few days before disturbing them again. Then on a good day we went up the hill once more, this time carrying all the film equipment. Again, we approached very openly and as soon as the bird slid off, we accelerated, reached the hide, Alan was pushed in with all his equipment, and we made sure he had everything and was settled, then I pushed off down the hill once more. We were in radio contact and from the floor of the glen, I asked if he was OK. Yes, everything was fine. Then another anxious wait and there was the bird slowly contouring back along the edge of the face then a swing out and on to the nest. No more radio contact. At the end of the day I would go up again and take him out.

Another open approach late that day. The bird went off at the same point I had reached on the hill the first time and I radioed Alan I was coming. He had of course seen me below and had everything ready for a quick exit. He was jubilant; he had taken great shots, he was so close he could hear the bird snapping twigs on the nest so he was unable to make much movement inside the hide and consequently was cramped and couldn't make good speed off the hill, even with me carrying most of the equipment. Back in the glen again, another careful watch, and there it was back on the nest. A great successful day at last.

The guiding season by then was almost upon us. I would be so busy with my clients, I would have very little time to spend with Alan, so Les was brought into the equation. He was always enthusiastic at whatever he did and we knew that he would be a very reliable back up. So I left for the first guiding week in Sutherland. The weather had been remarkably dry and a strong south-easterly wind blew right across the whole of the north-west Highlands. I particularly liked it in that quarter while I was in Sutherland for it usually meant very settled sunny days. Any showers that came in usually dropped their rain on the hills before they reached that far north-west corner so we were enjoying an excellent week.

Then sometime in the middle of the week, Norma phoned me from home. There was a massive brush fire very close to where the eagles were nesting, she hadn't heard from Alan or Les but it could be that they might be affected by this. A phone call to Alan in the evening confirmed our worst fears. He sounded so down that I didn't want to press him on details. We would meet as soon as

I returned on the Saturday. It appeared that all had been going extremely well. He and Les had set up a good rapport and they had a few days of good filming. Then mid-week Alan was in the hide and Les had gone home to get on with some painting. He had arranged to go back to take Alan out of the hide in the late afternoon. Meanwhile Alan was in his usual position and getting good footage of a change-over of birds in the nest. He glanced out of a side opening in the hide which allowed him to see down into the glen and saw a solitary figure approaching. This was not unusual, for walkers would often pass by oblivious of what was happening above. Then to his alarm this figure set fire to the heather some 500ft below Alan's position. This time of year was very often used by keepers for burning the old heather out, allowing new growth to come through which provides good feeding for young grouse later in the year. It's a practice which has gone on for many years but inevitably it can get out of hand, especially in conditions like these. The strong south-easterly wind fanned the flames and soon they were racing upwards. It was, without doubt, out of control and heading straight for Alan and the eagles. Soon the hide was filled with smoke, but Alan refused to budge, for all our work would be lost if he stepped outside, for without doubt the eagles would desert the nest if a figure suddenly appeared on the edge of the nest.

The fire brigade arrived, along with lots of local keepers who were trying to beat out the flames. They were of course totally ignorant of what was above them for we had kept so low a profile that as far as we knew, no one had any idea of what we were up to. With all this commotion, the sitting bird flew off the nest leaving the eggs uncovered and Alan finally emerged from the hide spluttering and headed down the hill with all his equipment. Les knew nothing of this disaster until he arrived to go up the hill to take Alan out and so he was very surprised to find him on the roadside waiting along with most of the fire services in Ross-shire while the hill continued to burn.

Our meeting over the weekend was very sombre. The fire had

subsequently been smothered but a watch on the nest confirmed our worst fears. The eagles had deserted. We would have to review the whole situation and have a look at our back-up nest to see at what stage the other pair were at.

The following week, I was working with my clients from our home base so Alan, Les and I went up to see how the other pair of eagles were faring in the evenings. By watching from a safe distance below, we could see that this pair were already bringing prey back to the nest. So the chicks were already hatched. This was another blow for Alan. There could now be no continuity. The nest of the first pair looked completely different to that of the back-up pair so there was no way a film editor could marry up footage of the eggs of the two pairs. He had hoped that if the back-up pair were still on eggs, we might just get a few shots before hatching, but the hope was snatched away. Alan had a long conversation with the film unit back at their base and it was decided that we should get all the useful footage we could for the remainder of the season and then try again the following year. So we set about the task of getting close to our second pair of birds.

Compared to the nest of our prime pair, this nest was a better proposition for setting up a hide. The downside was that the back-drop was not quite as good, for to see a bird come into the original nest was a very spectacular sight. This one, although good, was a little more limited in scope. However, we were prepared to make the most of it. We would try to set up a hide the next evening. All three of us were there for the setting up. Carrying everything we needed, we set off up the hill and saw one parent fly off. Working feverishly, we managed to find a good position where there was a clear view into the nest and a good view of the aerial approaches. We couldn't resist a quick look in to the cup and saw two chicks just a few days old before we ran downhill again and watched. The parent came back almost immediately and we went home reasonably happy.

Next day, since I was still quite busy, Les and Alan went back to see if Alan could get into the hide, for we had no time to lose now if there was to be an almost complete record of the chicks' development. They followed the usual routine of two going up openly and one coming down leaving the cameraman in the hide. They both waited and waited for one of the adults to come back and after some hours became very alarmed. Fortunately, they were in radio contact and Alan said he would have to come out for he thought the young chicks might get chilled. So Les made the journey up again and they returned to the floor of the glen, undecided as to what had gone wrong.

We all had a chat about this and someone came up with the idea that we had come across an eagle which could count. I was still too busy to join them at the eyrie to make up a third party but we had the idea of getting an old anorak and overtrousers, stuffing them with straw like a kind of scarecrow which Alan and Les could bounce up the hill between them, see Alan into the hide and Les would bounce the scarecrow back down the hill again. It worked. The eagle could count up to two but evidently not to three, and it returned to the nest almost immediately. Over the next several weeks Alan and Les were getting good footage of the family as they developed and since the chicks take about ten to 11 weeks before they leave that nest, Alan could take a few rest days from the hide where he went off to explore the area around looking for footage which might be useful in the finished film. When we had been doing our initial exploratory work, we had worked out the extreme edges of this pair's territory so that if we were watching them from a high position, we more or less knew at which point they would turn and come back towards us.

When I came back to Ross-shire one week in June, Alan said he had seen something unusual. He had been watching an eagle on the edge of the territory and, assuming it was one of our pair, it had not turned at its usual point but instead had wheeled and moved off away from the territory. We were both intrigued by this and decided to set up a watch the next evening further down the glen. This time it was a youngish eagle we saw. By its white markings we thought it might be about four years old. It flew to the edge adjoining our known bird's territory, then turned and flew over the back of the hill. Alan said it was not the bird he had seen last time. He had seen a fully grown adult.

I was still up to the eyes in work so he and Les decided to follow this up. They thought they would explore a side glen which led on to a flat plateau. It was an unlikely place to find an eyrie but they noticed an outcrop of rock which was no more than 30 to 40 feet high and on approaching realised there was an eyrie about halfway up the face. Rather than approach it, they sat at some distance and watched. Sure enough, an adult eagle arrived with prey which it deposited in the nest and flew off again. Then some distance away they saw the younger bird which was obviously the second of the pair. It looked very much like an older eagle had paired up with a much younger bird. On taking a quick look in the nest they saw two chicks at about the same stage of development as the two being filmed. It was decided that we should keep an eye on this to see what happened.

It was about this point that Alan had a call. He would have to leave, for he was required to start filming for a documentary about the Danube Delta. Les and I were sorry to see him go for he had become a very good friend and we hoped he would be back the following year to complete the eagle film. In the meantime, Les and I would continue to keep an eye on the young eagles until they left the nest successfully within the next two to three weeks.

By late June, our two eaglets were almost fully feathered, the head being the last to change from a downy white to a rich golden colour. They were constantly exercising their wings and flapping so hard at times they were in danger of knocking each other off the edge of the nest. They were doing so well that we thought we ought to leave them to their own devices and spend some time with the odd couple on the moorland eyrie. What we found worried us a great deal. From a vantage point to one side of the nest we could see the two chicks were surviving and were in about the same state of plumage as our birds in the other nest. But while our chicks were very lively and dancing around on the edge, these looked very listless. They lay motionless, heads towards the cliff and no interest in what was happening around them. We noted there was very little in the way of prey in the cup and we wondered if perhaps there was not enough of a territory for the adults to hunt efficiently.

We decided to set up a watch from some way off and try to estimate what, if anything, the adults were taking back for the youngsters. It soon became clear it was only the older bird who was taking any interest in the young chicks and doing all the hunting. The younger adult would put in an appearance occasionally but usually without prey. Would it be ethical to interfere with nature and try to do something to help? We thought about this for a while and decided we couldn't just stand by and do nothing. So next morning we got up very early, and drove around the local busier rural roads, stopping every so often to pick up any road kill we came across. Very soon we had a large plastic sack full of assorted dead animals, but mostly rabbits. We then drove down to our glen and walked up on to our plateau and the eyrie.

We knew full well we would have some problem delivering the goodies to the nest for, although there was a fairly low cliff, getting down from above would be very difficult as there was something of an overhang and climbing up from below would be laborious and slow. We had a climbing rope with us for any eventuality and we devised a method where, if I went on to the top above the nest, taking the bag of roadkill and the rope with me, I would be able to lower the various items of prey down on to the nest, guided by Les at our vantage point below, who would direct me to the right place – for I couldn't see the nest from above because of the overhang. There was no sign of the parent birds. We could see from the vantage point there was very little prey evident in the nest but at least one chick was standing while the other stared dejectedly into the cliff. On reaching the top, I unwound the rope and shook a rabbit out of the sack. Then, doubling the rope, I laid the rabbit carefully in the loop and lowered it slowly over the edge, looking to Les for guidance as to whether I should go left or right as it descended. To my great surprise, he was doubled up with laughter and he could hardly gesture one way or the other for a reason I couldn't understand. At last, despite a lack of instruction, I felt the rope go slack and assumed the rabbit was at its destination, so slowly pulled one end of the rope so that it might slip beneath the rabbit and pulled the rope to the top again. By this time, Les was climbing up to my position saying, 'You must let me lower the next one. The standing chick is a comedian. You must see what happens.' Mystified, I climbed down to the vantage point while Les was preparing the next rabbit. The standing chick was looking at nothing in particular and then this rabbit, its ears flapping slightly in the breeze, appeared over the overhang. The chick did a double take and watched, spellbound as this flying bunny slowly descended towards it. I too was having difficulty in giving directions for the expression on its face was incredible. Les's rabbit was very well aimed for it landed across the eaglet's talons. Then the end of the rope was dropped, falling just by the other chick, who was showing no interest whatsoever and gradually the rope-end was pulled through below the rabbit, the chick with its piercing eyes following every movement of the ascending rope-end until it disappeared above the overhang again. Then it looked down at its talons suddenly realising, 'You can actually eat this,' and started tearing into it.

So our routine was the same for the next few days, delivering as much roadkill as we could for the chicks. There was no doubt it made an amazing difference to their development. Very soon they were catching up on the other chicks in behaviour and animation. But one day we discovered the slower chick to be missing. We never found out what happened to it. It just disappeared. I would have to go off again with some clients and Les would have to get on with other things too. The chicks from the original nest had already flown successfully so we made a final journey back to the eyrie we were feeding with a particularly large sackful of roadkill and dumped it below the nest.

We were hoping there was enough there to encourage the

remaining chick to leave the nest or to see it through another few days if the parent could carry it in and then we left, hoping for the best.

In the course of the next winter, Norma and I found ourselves quite near the territory during a walk and we decide to get up on to the plateau so I could show her the odd position of the eyrie.

Most incredibly, we saw the unmistakeable markings of a first year eagle flying some way off. Was it the same chick? We shall never know but I like to think it was. The following year, Mike Richards took over where Alan had left off. By this time we were very busy with clients so I had little spare time. However before the season began, I brought Mike up to date on where we had spent so much of our efforts the previous year and had to leave him and Les to do all the work during that season. Happily, there were no disasters this time and the film was premiered in Eden Court Theatre in Inverness, I think around 1982.

Many people see the soaring eagle as a supreme emblem of freedom, and that is possibly why it features on so many national flags. None of us can ever achieve a degree of total personal freedom to compare with that, since we live in a society which requires that we conform to rules which make life bearable for all of us. But sometimes we can break the rules – or rather, break from other people's expectations of how we should lead our lives – make a leap in the dark, and – if we are fortunate – we can soar, free like the eagle.

Full circle, return to the Secret Howff

AS THE YEARS progressed, my early life in Aberdeen seemed very remote, I had lost the habit of visiting the Cairngorms – especially the eastern ones of my early days – and had lost touch with most, if not all, of my companions of that period. But life has a way of throwing up surprises...

It was sometime in the late 1980s that we decided to have a family Christmas in Braemar and during this time, my son Bruce and I wandered around some of my old haunts. One day we found ourselves in Glen Slugain and I thought I would show Bruce where we had built our Howff all those years ago when I was still in my teens, fully expecting to find just a heap of stonework. To my utter astonishment when we reached it, the Howff was in pristine condition. I couldn't believe it. I guessed that Charlie continued to use it after we had gone our separate ways. He never married, but he and one of Bob Scott's daughters had been linked for some time. I think it was she who, sometime in the early 1980s, had placed a stone above his ashes on a small island in the middle of the River Quoich. It was a favourite camping place for Charlie. The stone had a simple inscription: 'Charlie the Hiker.' I had no clue as to Doug's whereabouts as we had lost contact when I moved to the North West but I assumed he had moved away somewhere for work. So it looked very much as if a new generation had found it and not only used it but had made improvements. I was absolutely delighted that it had survived. Bruce and I found a log book in the Howff and we left a message for the caretakers to contact us if possible, but sadly no one did. For why should they? They were using it much as we had and like us were much too involved in doing the next climb or skiing to bother about its history which was only of marginal interest. For my part, I was still enjoying the winter work of setting up the places we would be visiting the following spring and summer. So the matter was largely forgotten.

It was when I was coming up to retirement, about a decade after the visit mentioned above, that my nephew Robin was reading Dave Brown and Ian Mitchell's book, *Mountain Days and Bothy Nights* and contacted me to say that he had read Ian's account of spending time in the Howff, but he thought Ian hadn't got the story of its history quite right. So I too read Ian's enjoyable book and discovered there were a few crossed wires which was understandable. My generation were of the opinion that their actions and exploits were of no interest to anyone else so didn't take the trouble of writing things down. To try and set the record straight, I wrote a letter to Ian's publisher where it languished for about six months, and then came a reply from Ian who had only then come across it. I was to discover that Ian was a stickler for accuracy in all he wrote. We arranged to meet and he sent my account of the building of the Secret Howff on to the Scottish Mountaineering Club who published it in their Journal in 1999. Ian and I became good friends, though neither of us had any idea of who exactly was putting in so much work to keep the howff in tip-top condition. Ian himself had left Aberdeen a decade after myself, and was unaware as to who the howff's present custodians were.

What I hadn't fully realised was that finding the Secret Howff had become something of a Holy Grail for some of the present generation of walkers, skiers and climbers. Everyone who found it became part of the conspiracy of keeping its whereabouts secret and felt part of the cognoscenti. It was agreed (but I don't know by whom) that no photographs or descriptions of its whereabouts would be published, but if you did find it, you were very welcome to use it. Such an emphasis on the howff being a 'secret' was not part of the intention of its original builders.

The year 2003 was the 50th anniversary of building the Howff and it occurred to me that it was time I should be trying to contact

Doug Mollison. Wouldn't it be great if we walked up there together 50 years after we had built it? A good friend of my elder brother had worked with Doug some years earlier and, though it was a slender chance, he was my only hope of regaining contact. Alas, it was too late. Doug had died in 2000. I felt my friends of youth should be remembered in some way for the pleasure they were still giving the present generation. The best way I could think of was to have a small brass plaque made with all the names involved in its construction and I arranged to meet Ian up at the howff, he travelling up from Glasgow and I down from the north. The plaque was duly screwed on to a building stone in the interior of the howff and we spent a pleasant day reminiscing of our younger climbing days with a couple of lads who had just come off Beinn a' Bhuird and had been using the howff overnight. Another consequence of my new friendship with Ian was that, though Ian's own contact with the eminent Canadian mountaineer, Chic Scott, I was able – when Ian went to give a talk at the Banff Mountain Book Festival in 2000 – to eventually re-establish contact with a couple of Aberdonian mountaineers, who had emigrated to Canada way back in the 1950s, 'Chesty' Bruce and 'Sticker' Thom, whom I had known back then, and who were now pals of Chic Scott!

A number of years later a radio programme was made about the howff in which both Ian and I took part, but once more it was still so secret that we still had no idea of who was actually looking after it and even in 2013, when my whole family and I walked up to the Howff for the 60th anniversary, we were still in the dark. Finally, it was decided, on the 50th anniversary of the Mountain Bothy Association, that a film should be made about all the bothies which were used by climbers over the years after the Second World War. In doing so, the filmmakers came across the group who were putting in all the work in maintenance of the Howff.

Once again we spent a day at the howff, where at long last we met one of the howff maintenance group, who we discovered spent several of their weekends carrying the necessary equipment and materials all the way up the glen to spend some very happy hours by the sound of it, doing whatever repairs were necessary to keep the doss going for yet another generation. In this way I found myself welcomed back into the fold of the climbing fraternity after a long absence – though in a sense, I had never been away, for I was simply continuing to enjoy the love and pleasure of Hill and Glen, albeit in a slightly different form, by taking others who so desired into our remote and wild places.

We were in the very vanguard of nature tourism. It was to be six or seven years before anyone else took up the idea of running natural history based courses and holidays. Generally, we were not welcomed with open arms by landowners and the Nature Conservancy, and it took some time for those bodies to catch up. We were regarded with some suspicion. So, on occasions, we had to contend with both the landowner, who didn't want us there at all, and the conservationists, who thought we would drive all the wildlife away. I am pleased to say that over the course of my lifetime, the position has been reversed. Our mountains are welcoming. Nature-based businesses are flourishing, mainly through a wider appreciation and knowledge of nature by the general public.

Long may this continue...

... and long may the Secret Howff remain a secret.

Mountain Days and Bothy Nights

Dave Brown & Ian R Mitchell
ISBN 978 1906307 83 7 PBK £7.50

This classic 'bothy book' celebrates everything there is to hillwalking; the people who do it, the stories they tell and the places they sleep, where bothies came from, the legendary walkers, the mountain craftsmen and the Goretex and gaiters brigade – and the best and the worst of the dosses, howffs and bothies of the Scottish hills.

This new edition brings a bit of mountaineering history to the modern Munro bagger. The climbers dossing down under the corries of Lochnagar may have changed in dress, politics and equipment, but the mountains and the stories are timeless.

Dave Brown and Ian R Mitchell won the Boardman Tasker Prize for Mountain Literature in 1991 for *A View from the Ridge*, the sequel to *Mountain Days & Bothy Nights*.

The Joy of Hillwalking

Ralph Storer

ISBN 978-1-842820-69-8 PBK £7.50

Hillwalking is only one of the passions in my life. In my experience, those who love the mountains are passionate people who are passionate about many things. That said, there are times, as I describe herein, when I simply have to go to the hills.

RALPH STORER

Ralph Storer's highly entertaining exploration of the lure of the hills is underpinned by hard-won experience – he has climbed extensively in the British Isles, Europe and the American West, though his abiding love is the Scottish Highlands. His breezy anecdotes of walking and climbing around the world in all sorts of conditions are gripping and full of fun. His sense of humour is as irrepressible as his relish for adventurous ascents, but he doesn't have his head in the clouds when it comes to serious issues such as public access and conservation.

The Ultimate Guide to the Munros

Ralph Storer

Volume 1: Southern Highlands	ISBN 978 1906307 57 8 PBK £14.99
Volume 2: Central Highlands South	ISBN 978-1-906817-20-6 PBK £14.99
Volume 3: Central Highlands North	ISBN 978-1-906817-56-5 PBK £14.99
Volume 4: Cairngorms South	ISBN 978-1-908373-51-9

From the pen of a dedicated Munros bagger comes *The Ultimate Guide* to everything you've wished the other books had told you before you set off. The lowdown on the state of the path, advice on avoiding bogs and tricky situations, tips on how to determine which bump is actually the summit in misty weather... this series forms the only guide to the Munros you'll ever need.

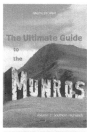
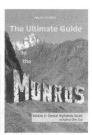
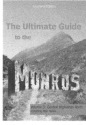
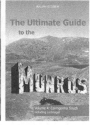

These comprehensive rucksack guides feature:

- Detailed descriptions of all practicable ascent routes up all the Munros and Tops in each region
- Easy to follow quality and difficulty ratings
- Annotated colour photographs and OS maps
- The history of each Munro and Top
- Notes on technical difficulties, foul-weather concerns, winter conditions and scenery

Winner of the highly commended Award for Excellence (for Vol. 1) by the Outdoor Writers and Photographics Guild

His books are exceptional... Storer subverts the guidebook genre completely.
THE ANGRY CORRIE

Irresistibly funny and useful... makes an appetising broth of its wit, experience and visual and literary tools. Brilliant.
OUTDOOR WRITERS AND PHOTOGRAPHICS GUILD

Details of these and other books published by Luath Press can be found at: **www.luath.co.uk**

Luath Press Limited
committed to publishing well written books worth reading

LUATH PRESS takes its name from Robert Burns, whose little collie Luath (*Gael.*, swift or nimble) tripped up Jean Armour at a wedding and gave him the chance to speak to the woman who was to be his wife and the abiding love of his life. Burns called one of 'The Twa Dogs' Luath after Cuchullin's hunting dog in Ossian's *Fingal*. Luath Press was established in 1981 in the heart of Burns country, and now resides a few steps up the road from Burns' first lodgings on Edinburgh's Royal Mile. Luath offers you distinctive writing with a hint of unexpected pleasures.

Most bookshops in the UK, the US, Canada, Australia, New Zealand and parts of Europe either carry our books in stock or can order them for you. To order direct from us, please send a £sterling cheque, postal order, international money order or your credit card details (number, address of cardholder and expiry date) to us at the address below. Please add post and packing as follows: UK – £1.00 per delivery address; overseas surface mail – £2.50 per delivery address; overseas airmail – £3.50 for the first book to each delivery address, plus £1.00 for each additional book by airmail to the same address. If your order is a gift, we will happily enclose your card or message at no extra charge.

ILLUSTRATION: IAN KELLAS

Luath Press Limited
543/2 Castlehill
The Royal Mile
Edinburgh EH1 2ND
Scotland

Telephone: 0131 225 4326 (24 hours)
email: sales@luath.co.uk
Website: www.luath.co.uk